A Portrait of PORTSEA
1840 - 1940

A Portrait of
PORTSEA
1840 - 1940

JOY HARWOOD

Ensign
PUBLICATIONS

First published in Great Britain in 1990 by
Ensign Publications
A division of Hampshire Books Ltd.,
2 Redcar Street
Southampton SO1 5LL

© Joy Harwood 1990.

Edited by David Graves.
Typeset by PageMerger, Southampton.
Jacket Design by Mark Smith.
Printed by Graficas London Ltd.

British Library Cataloguing in Publication Data
Harwood, Joy *1923 –*
    A portrait of Portsea 1840-1940.
    1. Hampshire. Portsmouth, history
    I. Title
    942.2792
ISBN 1-85455-044-6

CONTENTS

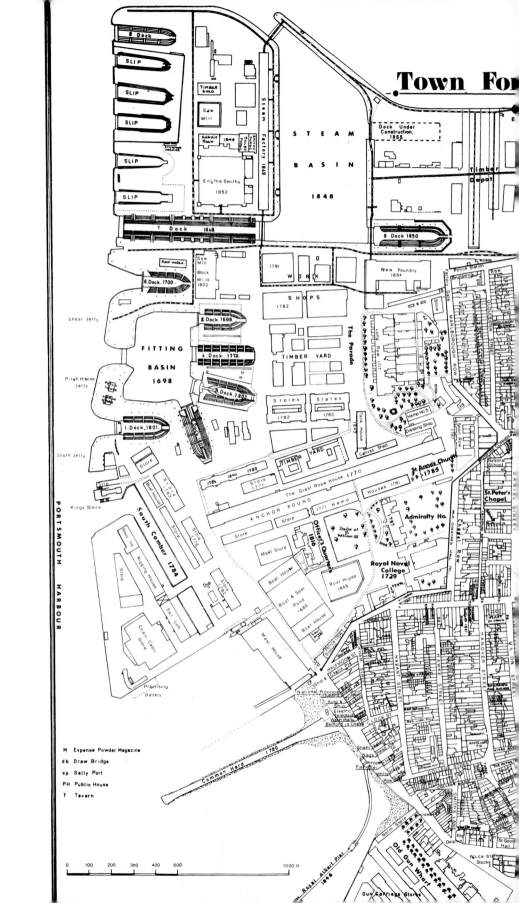

Town For

8 Dock

SLIP

SLIP

SLIP

SLIP

SLIP

TIMBER SHED

Saw Mill

Engine Room 1848

Steam Factory 1849

Engine Smithy 1852

STEAM BASIN 1848

Dock Under Construction. 1865

Timber Depot

7 Dock 1848

9 Dock 1850

Saw Mill

Pump House

Block Mills 1802

6. Dock. 1700.

1791

WORK

New Foundry 1854

Police Station

Shear Jetty

SHOPS 1782

Store

5. Dock. 1698.

Long Row 1717

FITTING BASIN 1698

4. Dock. 1772.

TIMBER YARD

The Parade

Pitch House Jetty

3. Dock 1803.

Hemp Ho 5

Stores 1782

Stores 1783

Dressing Shop

South Jetty

1. Dock. 1801.

Tank House 1783

Canvas Shed

St. Anne's Church 1785

Kings Stairs

Store 1863

Boat House

Stores 1819

Store

Store 1771

1786   1840   1789

TIMBER YARD

Houses 1781

National School

St. Peter's Chapel

The Great Rope House 1770

Admiralty Ho.

ANCHOR POUND

1771 Hemp

Statue of William III

South Camber 1784

Boat Ho

Rigging House

Store

Store

Store

Store 1782

Store

Meal Store

Officer's Quarters 1816

Boat House

Royal Naval College 1729

Chain Cable Store

Sail Loft

Boat & Spar Pond 1665

Boat House 1845

Boat House

PORTSMOUTH   HARBOUR

Practising Battery

Mast House

HALFMOON STREET

National Provincial Queen & Ship
King & Ship
Electric
Telegraph
Waterman
Bedford in Chase

LOCK ST

Sheer

Nags Head
Keppel Pier Hotel
White H
Row

Common Hard 1720

Royal Albert Pier 1848

North Street

Old Gun Wharf

Police Station

Gun Carriage Stores

M   Expense Powder Magazine

db   Draw Bridge

sp   Sally Port

PH   Public House

T   Tavern

0   100   200   300   400   500   1000 ft

PORTSEA

..ications & Royal Dockyard. (1860's)

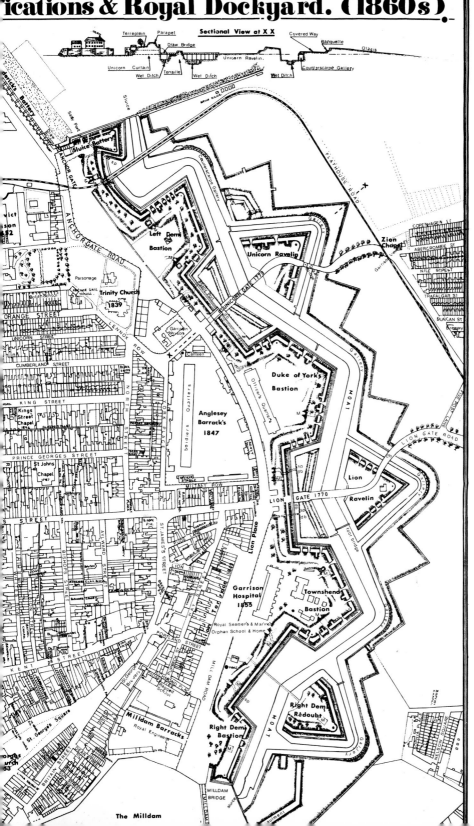

A PORTRAIT OF PORTSEA

"The town of Portsea now covers what was, within the last century, an extended waste ... generally known by the name of *Portsmouth Common*.

The town is divided by a very long street, called Queen-street, extending from the Dock to the Lion-gate, from which several streets pass to the Old Rope-walk in right angles, viz. Union, Bishop, and Hanover-streets, White's-row; to College-street, through the medium of Hawke and Havant-streets, and to Ordnance-row ... On the right-hand side of Queen-street is another part of Portsea, very extensive; consisting of many streets, known by the names of Daniel, Cross, North, Prince George's, King and Cumberland, with Chapel and Marlborough rows, consisting of private houses, and Frederick-street."

Henry Slight: *A Chronicle History of Portsmouth, 1868.*

← *Portsea, 1860s.*
(B.H. Patterson, 1976)

THE TURN OF THE CENTURY

The story of a city has to start somewhere, but if it is not to be from the very beginning, then where? If we are to tell about Portsea during the years 1840 to 1940 (and that is the intention) how far back must we go?

Perhaps it will prove sufficient to begin at the beginning of the nineteenth century, to set the scene as it then was, and in this introduction, to build upon the following forty years until we arrive at what should rightly be called page one.

The picture is one of harsh comparison between the activity and profit arising from war-time to the apathy and abject poverty of a peace-time community. There is a vivid account, written in 1795 by Dr. George Pinckard, who was in Portsmouth awaiting the departure of Sir Ralph Abercrombie's expedition to the West Indies: 'Portsmouth verifies to our experience all that we had heard of its unpleasantness and vulgar immodesty', he observed:

> The busy activity of the place occurs only ... when a fleet comes in or is about to sail, at which periods the town becomes all crowd and hurry for a few days, and then suddenly reverts to a languid intermission of dullness and inactivity.[1]

He is critical of the fact that 'the houses and lodgings have their war price and their peace price distinctly fixed', and that Portsmouth is 'not only filthy and crowded, but crowded with a class of low and abandoned beings'. He speaks of the 'riotous, drunken and immoral scenes,' of 'gross obscenity and intoxication', and he is upset above all by the 'hordes of profligate females seen reeling in drunkenness, or plying upon the streets in open day'.

His attack upon the street woman, the 'Sweet Poll of Portsmouth' contrasts vividly with his later appreciation of the Dockyard, the Navy in general, in particular the men who man the ships. One could perhaps question the character of Dr. Pinckard himself: was he rather too puritan, too well-established and comfortable in his own environment to have even a grain of sympathy for those 'languishing nymphs'? They were, he says:

> ... of more than Amazonian stature, having a crimson countenance ... wounded cheeks, a tumid nose, scarred and battered brows, and a pair of blackened eyes ... callous to every sense of shame, these daring objects reel about the streets ... like the devouring Kite ... eager to pounce upon their prey; and each unhappy tar, who has the misfortune to fall under their talons, has no hope of escape till plucked of every feather.

By comparison with this outburst against the backstreet prostitutes of Portsmouth, Dr. Pinckard says his visit to the Dockyard 'was of a nature highly gratifying', adding, 'I contemplated this vast depot of stores – this great workshop of our Navy, as the emblem of our nation's glory'. He speaks with admiration of the damage caused to the recently captured French ship *Tigre* by the 'thunderbolt of Britain'. And of his visit to Haslar Hospital, he says:

> Too much cannot be done for our Navy, nor can the provision of our sick and wounded defenders be too liberal; ... *they are a race of heroes!* [2]

Whether seen through the enthusiastic eyes of Dr. Pinckard, or the blackened eyes of 'Sweet Poll', the value of the Navy was certainly recognised by the community, particularly at a time when the French were breathing down the British neck; and it was largely due to preoccupation with the war and, to a lesser extent, the French Revolution that a new influence, Catholicism, began to make itself felt in the area.

Priests fleeing from France found sanctuary on this side of the Channel and, regarded at first with some suspicion, the Catholic church began to grow in strength in Portsea; centred first on a chapel in Unicorn Row, it progressed over the century to the Cathedral which opened its doors in 1882, at the same time benefitting the community with the building of eighteen more churches, of orphanages, schools and even a Home for Penitents.

By contrast, St. George's Church had been part of the community since 1752, when the Town Fathers had agreed to the building of a new church, St. Mary's being a long way from Portsea and the walk too much for the elderly and infirm. The people themselves raised the money, and the work was undertaken by fifteen shipwrights from the Dockyard, assisted by 'three gentlemen, one carpenter, one tallow chandler and one grocer'.

But in 1800 there was little comfort for the common man. '1800 was, perhaps, the saddest year Portsmouth had ever experienced'[3] for prices were exceptionally high and the shortage of food acute. On 6 January, 'the bakers close their ovens and refuse to bake bread, in order to induce the Magistrates to raise the assize of that article'; in September there was a 'tumultous meeting of the populace in St. George's Square, Portsea, respecting the high price of bread; many windows broken and other damage done'. Such were the conditions that by 13 December, 'provisions (were) so scarce that servants were allowed only one quartern loaf of brown bread per week, and nine hundred pounds collected in Portsmouth to purchase Scotch herrings to supply the poor'.[4]

King's Mill, originally established to provide the armed services, had been turned over to supplying the people of Portsmouth and Portsea, but this was only possible in peace-time, and over the years the population was constantly agitating for an improvement in the supply and price of basic food items.

It would be years before these protests were heard, but in common with many other authorities throughout the country, the Town Council was driven at last to make some positive move, and in 1841 it was agreed that a petition be sent to the Government observing that 'the deplorable and suffering condition of the great mass of the people requires the laws concerning the importation of corn to be altered'.[5]

A year later, in August 1842, a Hampshire farmer voiced his opinion on the subject in a letter to the press:

> The thanks of the community are especially due to you for dragging forth to public notice the barefaced extortion now practised in reference to the price of bread ... (which) has for many years been far too high as compared with the price of wheat...
>
> Calculating by the price of flour alone, the sack of wheat, when converted into flour, is charged to the public 36s 3d. whereas I, the grower, receive only 27s., so that the profit of the miller and baker on four bushels is 9s 3d., or more than one third of the value!...
>
> Most happy should I be to see some of the above gentry come forward and attempt to vindicate themselves from the charges of imposition ... I am, sir, yours respectfully,
>
> A. FARMER[6]

'Un-English, arbitrary, and despotic in its character', the Press-gang was perhaps the greatest threat to the well-being of the population as they scoured the streets of Portsmouth in the early years of the century, sweeping up every able-bodied man they could lay hands on. There was no consideration given to family circumstances, so that even though a man might leave behind a widowed mother or a wife and several children, there was no appeal against the five or six years of compulsory service ahead of him.

On 23 September, 1803, there appeared an account of a 'very hot press' which took place in Portsmouth, Portsea and Gosport. '... no protestations were listened to, and a vast number of persons were sent on board the different ships in this port'. However, according to one report not all these raids were a complete success:

> Most were this morning liberated, being master tradesmen, apprentices, and such persons; very few were detained in comparison with the number taken on board. On the whole it is not supposed the service acquired 50 serviceable men.

Sometimes the authorities would even resort to trickery, as in the case of a Captain Bowen who marched a party of marines to Monckton Fort, ostensibly to quell a riot; many hundreds of people turned out to see the fun, only to find the marines had been posted at the end of Haslar Bridge with orders to round up every man who fitted the Captain's requirements. In this underhand fashion they made what was considered to be the finest haul on record.[7]

The Dockyard has always been at the centre of life on Portsea Island, employing directly or indirectly the vast majority of working men in the area. In the years that followed the Napoleonic Wars there was still a permanent military garrison in the town and this, combined with the steady flow of sea-going men, meant that most families were dependent for survival on various aspects of the nation's defence.

Development spread out from Old Portsmouth and Portsea as the population increased more rapidly than anywhere in the county, first toward Landport and Kingston, then to the outlying farming communities of Froddington, Milton and Eastney, finally – to cope with the novelty of seaside holidays and sea-bathing – taking in Southsea.

A reliable supply of good clean water began to reach into most areas of the town, gas lighting appeared on the streets as early as 1823. The Arundel Canal, opened in the same year, held out promise of trade expansion, but hopes faded as it was discovered to be polluting the water supply; freight charges went up so much as to make it no longer profitable, and by 1900 it had been abandoned.

The brewing industry was expanding rapidly, offering work prospects for many, and the arrival of the railway in 1847 encouraged businessmen in the clothing trade to develop what was already a promising corset industry. With a large number of available women, wives and widows of service men in desperate need of money, the opportunities for growth would eventually make this one of the three main industries in the town.

While building and development was reaching out in every direction, the original areas around Portsea and Old Portsmouth remained very much the same, the poorer houses deteriorating rapidly for want of the finance to improve or replace them. There were dark and narrow 'courts' huddled behind the busy shops of Queen Street and the spacious elegance of St. George's Square and Lion Terrace, and these courts housed people, six or seven to a family, crammed in to two or three small rooms, dependent on the limited amount of work available, ill-fed and poorly clothed. Their babies died in infancy, there was little or no education for the older children, and for the elderly there was often nothing but the workhouse. Common to any seaport, there was prostitution and vice at nearly every corner, the only saving grace the very real sense of community that existed from house to house, court to court and street to street.

All these factors – the Dockyard, the breweries, the coming of the railway and the failure of the Canal – all these, and war and peace and the threat of more war, affected the Common Man of Portsea, mostly to his detriment. He faced the 1850s with little to look forward to, and much to fear.

Queen Street and Dockyard Main Gate
(Portsmouth City Museum)

PART I

CITY CINDERELLA

The young Queen Victoria, crowned only two years before, was married in 1840, and for at least one day in the year the poor were to forget the squalor of their situation as they joined in the celebrations. A general holiday had been declared, there was to be feasting for all, and to add to the day's celebration church bells rang, guns were fired in loyal salute and by night ships in the harbour were illuminated. As one commentator observed, 'in a word all went as merry as a marriage bell'[1].

It was not often that the poor of the town had much cause for rejoicing; for the vast majority employment was scarce or at best intermittent, particularly for those in the Dockyard who were almost totally dependent upon the vagaries of war. There was little or no education for the children and for the most part housing was totally inadequate.

Portsmouth Town had long outgrown the fortifications which surrounded it, making for appalling overcrowding that resulted in conditions similar to those in Messum's Court:

> Many of these courts were closed at both ends and approached by covered passages, and in them the filth flooding from privies and the refuse thrown by the inhabitants accumulated. In some there were only one tap and one privy to serve as many as sixty people. Such was Messum's Court, situated below sea-level and therefore very damp, reached from a narrow street below the town walls known as Prospect Row (which has now become Gun Wharf Road) and through a tunnel only two feet wide which was called Squeeze-Gut Alley. Here 116 people lived, some of them in cellars, with one privy between them and one standpipe which supplied water for perhaps ten minutes a day. Through the court ran a large open drain as well as an open midden and when this was

> emptied the contents would remain for three days on the surface.[2]

This massive overcrowding had resulted in the initial overspill to Portsmouth Common, later to become Portsea; but now, by the middle of the nineteenth century, Portsea itself had increased its population by two-thirds and was rapidly outgrowing its housing capability. While there was little or no building going on, the population had increased by some 3,500, resulting in considerable overcrowding and the increased risk of disease.

As little more than a gesture, the Council showed its concern by making an official protest to Parliament about the Window Tax, which was described as 'unjust in its nature, unequal in its operation, and highly injurious in its effects'. It was claimed that in many of the poorer districts such a tax resulted in the reduction of light and air in what were already squalid houses, '. . . and is consequently one of the greatest hindrances to the amelioration of their sanitary condition'.[3]

To make matters worse, it was at this period that the Navy was making its slow transition from sail to steam, resulting in expansion and a demand for more land to be taken into the Dockyard; to this end the Admiralty acquired an area of some seven acres in Portsea known as New Buildings, thus further restricting the area available for housing.

The purchase of New Buildings also meant that Portsea was now cut off from the harbour, except at The Hard, a most notorious area that became the subject of much discussion and protest.

In 1858 two hundred inhabitants signed a petition, complaining of drunk and disorderly conduct on the part of the soldiers and sailors, marines and prostitutes who 'infested' the area, apparently without let or hindrance:

> The scenes which are to be witnessed here are of the most revolting description. They cannot fail to excite feelings of astonishment and disgust (and) such a state of things has reached a height barely endurable. When a ship happens to be paid off in the port, these evils are increased tenfold. The Hard then presents a scene of drunkenness and profligacy which baffles all description.[4]

Little was done to repair such a reputation, but eventually word reached the House of Commons where, in 1895, the Chancellor of the Exchequer was heard to give a most unfavourable report to the Members concerning the licensed premises on The Hard. Although he did not actually put a name to the area, undoubtedly 'the cap fitted':

> In one of our great towns there is a street containing twenty-

seven houses and having a length of 191 yards; and this is the way in which the houses are used; No.1 is a public-house; No.6 is a public-house; No.7 a beer house; No.8 a public-house; No.9 a public-house; No.10 a public-house; No.11 a Post Office.

He went on to reveal that Nos.12 and 13 were also public-houses, No.14 a wine and spirit store, Nos.16, 18, 21, 23 and 24, public-houses – and No.20 was an hotel.

That is the number of houses that the Magistrates have licensed. . . in spite of the remonstrances of some of the inhabitants of the street . . . I do not consider that anyone can think that a satisfactory state of things.[5]

In a letter to the *Evening News*, a reader lists the names of some of these public houses, as he recalls them from 1886; they included the Ship and Castle at No.1; *Queen's Head*, 7; *London Tavern*, 8; *King and Queen*, 9; *Ship Anson*, 10; *Victoria and Albert*, 11; *Waterman's Arms*, 13; *Bedford in Chase*, 14; *Sheer Hulk*, 19; *Nag's Head*, 21; *Keppel's Head*, 24-25; *White Hart*, 27; *Row Barge*, 30; and the *Earl of St. Vincent* at No.31.

By way of protest at the Chancellor's remarks – or maybe in justification – it was pointed out that the Chancellor either did not know or had decided not to mention that the assorted licensed premises were not there for the convenience of the local inhabitants, rather for 'the thousands of dockyardmen, sailors, visitors and passengers to and from Gosport, who used The Hard every day'. Fifty years before the area was 'occasionally the scene of disorder', but since then it had become 'as orderly and respectable as any reasonable being could desire'.

For whatever reason, by mid-century those who could afford to had begun to move outward, away from Portsea to Landport and Kingston, and to the new and elegant suburb of Southsea. But there were those who chose to remain, among them the more fortunate Naval and Dock-yard families who lived in the areas of St. George's Square and Lion Terrace, staying on in their well-designed, dignified and spacious houses, splendidly isolated from the squalor of the courts and alleys only yards away.[6]

But for the people living in Blossom Alley, White's Row and other, similar black spots the conditions, already appalling, deteriorated steadily; some would make courageous attempts to alleviate the worst aspects of poverty, and indeed one observer commented that 'little houses without bathrooms do not necessarily make slums'. Contrary to the accepted idea of poverty and hardship, this same observer comments upon the 'obvious pride and neighbourly competition' in the

Pavement

Wickham Street

Pavement

Gulley

Building 23 feet high

No.1 No.2 No.3 No.4 No.5 No.6 No.7 No.8 No.9

Tap

Godden's Court

Surface Gutter

Yard

Wall 11 feet high

Gutter

Building 17 feet high

Wall 11 feet high

Ground Plan of Godden's Court, between Wickham Street and Havant Street, showing nine of the twelve dwellings in this one closely confined area. (PCRO 114A/1/3/2/14) holystoning of a front-door step, a cosy picture of the Englishman's Castle extending even to the mean alleyways that led off Queen Street – so dreary in contrast to Queen Street itself, 'bright with shops of all sorts'.[7]

The *Hampshire Telegraph* reporting on the 'fatal affray' in White's Row voiced the more general opinion at the time, calling upon the authorities to suppress the 'dens of infamy' that existed in that neighbourhood; it was not, however, until some fifty years later that the Corporation took action to sweep away the tenement houses, the brothels and the many beer houses, to lay out new roads and council homes built to a standard that is still, in many cases, acceptable today.

Tea Kettle Alley, later known as Camden Alley, was one of the first to be demolished:

> Camden Alley was a trap for the unwary. It was situated at the Dockyard end of Queen Street and was formed by a triangular block of buildings which obstructed the main road at the spot. Narrow and ill-lighted it was the resort of itinerant vendors of wonderful watches, pipes, chains and jewels of all descriptions which dire poverty alone compelled them to part with at one-tenth of their value. Many a simple-minded sailor was had in this way, paying high prices for worthless rubbish. . .[8]

This highly undesirable area disappeared beneath a new roadway system, and over the years others were to follow, such as Rosemary Lane and 'one of the chief haunts of vice', Victory Road.

In 1906 Alderman T. Scott Foster was made a Freeman of the town. In his speech of acknowledgement he said that when he first entered public life, thirty years before, there had been as many as eight people living in one house, but the situation had so improved that at the time of speaking there were now only five:

> . . . at the earlier time they had no fire brigade; there was no sanitary staff worthy of the name, no hospital for infectious diseases, no asylum, no park or recreation ground, no museum, no library, no public baths and the elementary schools were very few.[9]

An 'Official Representation'

However, if things did look marginally better, as far as housing was concerned the first real and positive move toward slum clearance did not take place until 1909, when Dr. A. Mearns Fraser, the Medical Officer of Health, addressed his 'Official Representation to the Mayor,

Alderman and Burgesses', under the Housing of the Working Classes Act.

In this Report he drew attention to 'the narrowness, closeness, bad arrangements and . . . condition of the streets and houses . . . , together with the want of light, air, ventilation and proper convenience'.

He went into some detail about the area involved, commenting on the lack of any previous attempt to improve conditions, and saying that in 1903 the Corporation had turned down a proposal for improvement on the grounds of the expense involved.

'At that time,' he stated, '. . . there were in the area 198 properties consisting of dwelling-houses together with some mission halls, slaughter-houses, stables, stores, etc.' Since that date, many of the premises had been purchased by the Corporation and demolished to make way for street widening; but in May 1908, as a result of a house-to-house inspection, he had observed that there were still 435 inhabitants in a total of 107 occupied houses:

> All these houses are old and dilapidated, and the streets are so narrow that it is impossible for a sufficient circulation of fresh air to take place. Very many of the houses are of the back-to-back type, they are without damp-courses, without washhouses, without separate water closets, without ash bins, without separate water supplies, and generally damp, dark, ill-ventilated and originally of faulty construction.

Southampton Row, he went on, was 627ft. long and 7½ft. wide, while under the existing law a street over 100 ft. long was required to be at least 40ft. wide. It is perhaps surprising that he did not draw attention to King's Bench Alley, the measurements of which were even less acceptable – 586ft. long, with an average width of 3-4ft., the width at both entrances being less than 4ft.

He had satisfied himself that few of the occupied houses were tenanted by *bona fide* working class people, and he had found evidence of at least fourteen brothels.

In such conditions it was hardly surprising that the mortality rate for the area was some 2½ times greater than in the rest of the Borough; Dr. Mearns Fraser put the blame for this on the unhealthy and insanitary conditions, which resulted in one third of the deaths being from tuberculosis, while many children died in the first two years of life from gastric and intestinal illnesses. In the course of his investigations he had invited the Poor Law Medical Officer, Dr. McEwan, to investigate the situation for himself, and he fully corroborated the opinion of Dr. Mearns Fraser that the conditions were 'dangerous to health and cannot be remedied otherwise than by an Improvement Scheme for the rearrangement and reconstruction of streets and houses within the area'.[10]

Although the scheme was approved on 25 October 1910, it was to be nearly two years before the Borough of Portsmouth, under Part I of the Housing of the Working Classes Act, 1890, made an Order confirming an Improvement Scheme, in which the Local Authority 'resolved that the area described . . . is an unhealthy area and made a Scheme . . . for the improvement of that area'.

It was planned to purchase the whole of the 'Unhealthy Area', with the exception of certain houses which had been converted into store-houses and were therefore not part of the Scheme. The area involved, approximately 2½ acres, formed a rough rectangle bounded by parts of Queen Street on the North, Kent Street to the South, in the East King's Bench Alley and to the West, by Southampton Row, plus two pieces of land in White's Row. All the houses within this area were to be demolished by the Council with a Reconstruction Scheme to follow.

The principles of the Scheme were:

> 1. To provide a good wide thoroughfare, bright and attractive to look at, and healthy and pleasant to live in. . . incidentally transforming the worst conglomeration of slum property in the Borough with a model working-class residential neighbourhood.
> 2. To secure as large a number of good working-class houses, at moderate rents, as can, with due regard to health and amenity, be placed upon the area.
> 3. To provide an open space, planted with trees, which shall be a lung for the neighbourhood, and afford a play ground for the children.

It was intended that the area should not only be a healthier place to live in, but that it should also be pleasing to the eye. The road, therefore, was to be wide and straight, with pavements, while 'the outlines of the sides of the roads are broken to avoid dullness', trees were to be planted on both sides – ' the provision of forecourts to the houses render this possible without darkening the front rooms . . .'.

The forty-six two-storied houses to be built were described as 'ordinary self-contained cottages', provided for 'members of the working-classes displaced by the Scheme'. Each cottage was to have a garden, in some cases 45ft. long, and the Council went to some lengths to explain that although this may be considered excessive, it was unavoidable, the depth concerned (210ft.) being too narrow for two streets, but wider than was necessary for one. Furthermore, all but four looked on to the open space provided for the children.

By the standards of the day, these cottages were generous in their accommodation; there were three quite similar designs, one of these having 5 rooms, a scullery and a W.C., a living room (10½ft. x 9ft.) with

St. George's Church, Portsea
(Pen and ink drawing by Deane Clarke, October 1978)

Foundation stone laid on 24th October 1912 by Alderman Sir Scott Foster, J.P.
(City Secretariat, Portsmouth)

a bay window, and a kitchen (11½ft. x 12ft.) There was to be a bath in the scullery, filled from the nearby copper, plus a larder and a place for coal under the stairs. The drainage was to run out from the back, rather than under the house to the road.

In the final paragraph of the Order, it is observed that, while there were 130 people to be rehoused:

> The total accommodation provided for persons of the work-ing-classes, all 5 persons to each dwelling-house, is for 230. It is not proposed therefore to provide any further accommoda-tion outside the area included in the Scheme.

The cost involved is laid out in some detail, even to the 'amount estimated to be realised by the sale of old materials, say £260', making a grand total of £14,893.[11]

With some positive progress now being made, Dr. Mearns Fraser submitted a further Report in which, with a considerable degree of satisfaction, he was able to claim that 'there is an absence of tenement houses, and the working classes reside in self-contained cottages, a large proportion owning their own houses'.[12]

Homes for Heroes

The First World War would have brought such redevelopment to a standstill, but with the Armistice and the return of service men eager to set up home, the Government recognised the need for a vast and immediate national housing scheme. The idea of 'Homes fit for Heroes' caught the imagination, just as it was intended to do, but the underlying motive was more sinister than altruistic – it was almost the only weapon available for the use of the Government against the very real threat of post-war revolution. After the signing of the Armistice, there was every indication that soldiers returning from the war would be filled with the same bitter sense of unrest as had affected Russia and Germany.[13] Unemployment and poor living conditions awaited these men, and, knowing it was unable to subdue by force an army of some five million, the Government resorted to persuasion, beginning with a go-ahead housing scheme.

The birth of the 'Garden City' movement, with its tree-lined streets and spacious gardens, offered a semi-rural standard of middle-class housing such as the pre-war city dweller could scarcely imagine. But the good intentions of 1919 were hampered by financial interests and with the slump in 1920-21, progress was in danger of coming to a standstill. But the urgent need for housing remained, and at least the idea of the municipal garden suburb persisted, setting a level of design that was sustained throughout the 1920s and 30s.

The Garden City scheme had begun to take shape back in 1887 with the Lever brothers moving their factory from Warrington to a site on Merseyside; there they built a village for the workers, not so much out of goodness of heart but in the interest of industrial relations. By the turn of the century the Quaker Cadbury family had followed the Lever example, though George Cadbury's motives were somewhat different:

> I know the Birmingham housing question by visiting men in their houses in the city, and I have had the great privilege of reforming many hundreds of drunkards there. The question that came to me was, 'What have you to offer the working-man in the evening except the public house?', and this was the answer I arrived at: 'The most legitimate occupation is for them to come back to the land' . . .
> I can see no other way of saving England, for if a man works in the factory by day and sits in the public house by night, what can you expect but a poor emaciated creature without physical or moral strength?[14]

The Garden City scheme arrived in Portsmouth with the proposals put forward by Councillor Spickernell, designed to tackle the housing problem for men returning from the war.

There were some who considered it a grandiose scheme, to build a Garden City on the slopes of Portsdown Hill, for the project involved the building of some four hundred houses. However, land was acquired from Captain Thistlethwayte of Southwick, and estimates were submitted at an average cost of £900 each house. This was considered to be rather high, but it was pointed out that the price compared favourably with those in the rest of the country, and building went ahead. For some time it was referred to as 'Spickernell's Folly', but in the years that followed, it proved to be only the forerunner of vast development outside the town boundary, at Wymering in 1919, and at Eastney in 1920.

Even so, with all the building and with so many families rehoused, there were still many who had nowhere to go, and in May and June 1921, more than one thousand local people made a formal appeal through the *Evening News* that was to result in the Housing Committee redoubling its efforts over the coming years. In particular there was evidence of a determined effort to rid Portsea of its slums once and for all. There was the problem that, given the choice, some people would rather have stayed on where they were, presumably because the devil they knew was better than a move to Cosham, but by 1927 even the notorious Blossom Alley seemed set for demolition.[15]

Blossom Alley, 1927

There appear to have been seventeen houses in the Alley at this time, many of them the property of a Mrs. J. Humphries of Grove Road, Southsea. Some were three-roomed houses, occupied by single people, but in No.9, in three similar rooms, there was a family of ten – the husband and wife, two children over twelve years and six under twelve. Their accommodation consisted of two rooms on the ground floor, one on the first floor with some sort of attic or roof space above, and the largest of these rooms being 13½ft. x 10ft. x 6¾ft.

An Inspector's report[16] on the condition of this house is common to most of those in Blossom Alley. Circulation of air was described as 'bad, with no through ventilation', and no damp course was visible. In its favour, it did have running water and mains drains, the refuse was collected twice a week, and there was a flush toilet in the back-yard 'in fair condition'.

The general condition, however, gave some cause for alarm: the chimney stack leaned, the walls were fractured, and the upper floors and roof were shored up. Internally the stairs were shaky, and the tenant had had to erect a wooden partition to make a sleeping area for the six children.

Although this inspection was carried out in May 1927 it was not until the end of December that the house was submitted to the Health and Housing Committee as unfit for human habitation. A Closing Order was made as a result of a visit by the Committee in January 1930, and a further eight months elapsed before it was demolished by the owner as a result of a Council Demolition Order.

Mr. Eastman, the tenant, had been paying 5s. a week for this place; he was willing to move the family to any part of the City – except Cosham – and he felt able to pay an extra 1s. a week for better accommodation, but he could not offer more since he was not in regular employment.

In some of these houses, the rooms were so small as to be little more than cupboards, as indicated in the Inspector's note relating to No.13:

> Complete Inspection . . . cannot be made at present owing to illness. Mrs. Phillips is lying seriously ill in front room on ground floor. The bed being so situated that there is no access to staircase.

Further down the Alley, at No.17, seven people shared the two rooms and an attic, and in spite of this limited accommodation, the occupier 'kept four fowls'. The gas cooker was in the cellar and:

> . . . considerable trouble is caused by bugs in this property these apparently emmerge (*sic*) from cracks and defective portions of plaster.

This tenant, too, was willing to go 'anywhere in the City except Cosham'. No reason is given for this objection, though living there would mean a long journey to work, and presumably Cosham would have appeared to be in the depths of the outback to someone used to such a confined area as Portsea.

In nearby Frederick Street, the Inspector reported that the cellars were dirty and damp:

> . . . The gas cookers are fixed in the cellars and close to same the refuse receptacles are kept. The gully trap connections to drain are situated a considerable distance from draw taps thus causing the floor of cellar to be more or less always wet. The Water Closets are a considerable source of trouble owing to being open to the public.

There was one house, No.4 Hewlings Court (from Cross Street) which was reported to have fractured walls which leaned outward; the roof was subsiding, and the ceiling of the top room was bulging to the extent of about 1ft. 'This has been shored up but the timber is of insufficient strength to be of any use'. As a final note, 'the tenant of this house uses cellar. The only access to same is by means of flap at front. There are no stairs'. Although the building was specifically described as being in a dangerous condition, the tenant, a widow, had no wish to move to a better house. She could only afford 5s. a week and was anxious to remain in Portsea.

There were a dozen or so houses in St. George's Passage, Kent Street, all of which were in a similar state of disrepair. Originally built back-to-back with houses in Kent Place, the latter had been demolished some years before, leaving the rear walls of St. George's Passage exposed to the elements. Furthermore, the water closets in the cellars were in 'direct communication' with the dwelling houses. 'Refuse receptacles, water taps and gas cooker (sic) are also in cellars which are dirty and damp'.

Something in the region of 150 houses were inspected at this time, in York Place, Taylor Court (off Britain Street), Victoria Place (from Havant Street), North Street and Chatham Row (off North street). Of one of these, the Inspector commented that only two rooms (of six) are used, the rest being 'unfurnished, dirty and dilapidated'. The back bedroom of No.72 North Street was situated over the kitchen of No.73, and in another, the family of four was 'unable to use bedrooms as they are infested with vermin i.e. bugs and fleas'. In Hawke Street, the only brickwork at No.33 was the scullery and flues to the fireplace; the rest was made of lath and plaster with wooden partitions, and 'considerable nuisance is caused by rats, their runs being in the lath and plaster partitions'.

In one house in York Place there are two couples, Mr. and Mrs. Bryden and Mr. and Mrs. Stagg, as well as a Mr. Hunt and a Miss Pobjoy, all living in just six rooms, the rent being 11s. 9d. inclusive; and in the five rooms at No.15 York Place, there are two married couples, a Mrs. Vallor, a Mr. Miller, a 'cat, a dog and fowls'.

Some of these houses were to be demolished, some purchased by the Council, while on some a decision had yet to be taken, but with all of them there is no mention in the Report of any adverse reaction to the Demolition Orders; in almost every case there is a note that the owner was persuaded to demolish where ordered so to do, and that within a matter of months.

A difficult situation was further aggravated in 1929 when a number of men were drafted to Portsmouth from Rosyth and Pembroke Dockyards; but in this instance the Admiralty was persuaded to take a hand, allocating land to the north of Portsea Island on which houses were to be built for these men and their famililes.[17]

In 1935 the problem of housing in Portsea was still unresolved, and at a meeting in March, chaired by Councillor Spickernell, an attempt was made to arrive at a 'settled lay-out for the Portsea district, having regard to the proposals for clearance areas'.

Various suggestions were made, including plans for Queen Street to become a 'wide, tree-lined boulevard and shopping centre leading to the Hard that would be a thing of beauty instead of a paradise for mudlarkers'.[18] Kent Street was to continue into St. George's Square, and the construction of a road was planned to pass through Daniel Street into Queen Street; the Colllege Street area was to be enlarged, and Cumberland Street was to be reconstructed to improve access to adjoining streets.

It was proposed that the Admiralty be approached with a view to the Council purchasing land in the Bonfire Corner area, but at their next meeting members of the Special Joint Committee were informed that the Admiralty had rejected this suggestion.

At the same meeting, the Queen Street project began to take shape. The street was to be widened to 50ft., and plans were approved to acquire properties on the north side for the building of shops with flats over. This would do away forever with the proposal that the Dockyard take in the stretch of land north of Queen Street, leaving a strip undeveloped to provide access for 'any future tunnel to Gosport'.

That 'arch enemy of slumdom', Dr. Mearns Fraser, was still Medical Officer of Health after thirty-eight years in the post, and in recognition of his services he was invited to perform the opening ceremony of a new block of flats erected on the corner of Britain Street and Sun Street. Called, appropriately enough, Fraser House, this block together with its twin, Brunel House, was further evidence of the Council's determination to complete its five-year clearance scheme.[19] In December of the following year plans were submitted for flats to be built in Cumberland Street and with a view to the future, the street was to be widened to 40ft. with sufficient land retained to widen still further to 60ft., should the need arise.

It was recognised that all this building was going to displace over thirteen hundred people, and to meet their needs 425 flats were to be erected in a number of areas including Kent Street, Havant Street and Victory Road. By August 1937 the scheme was extended still further, to take in areas of Southsea and Landport, and to include 139 dwellings which would be erected in Cosham.

With the aim of making the area as pleasing as possible, Ranwell's Court in Portsea was to be used, temporarily, as a children's playground, and the Committee agreed that, with the lack of any recreational facilities, provision of permanent playgrounds should be considered along with the rest of the development.

Throughout the months leading up to the Second World War, there was talk of improvement to The Hard and its immediate surroundings; the City Engineer submitted a plan for the alteration to the railway line, there were plans for a new viaduct for rail traffic into the Dockyard, of turning facilities for trolleybuses and of a small yacht harbour. It was proposed that a portion of land recently reclaimed might include a bathing pool and a children's playground, while, in an effort to provide better facilities for the young, the Portsmouth and District Free Church Women's Council applied for the use of No.147 Queen Street as a club for local boys and girls. Unfortunately this had to be turned down as the premises were included in the road-widening project.

As far back as 1934 Councillor Spickernell was reported as saying that his dream of a new Portsea 'might take fifty years. . . it might take a hundred. But that did not matter much, so long as, sooner or later, it was accomplished'. He held on to a vision of the Hard being transformed with ornamental gardens, with a bandstand and tennis courts, and a promenade overlooking a small yacht haven. :

> . . . the people of Portsea did not want to be transported to Hilsea, Cosham and other spots on the outskirts. And if they didn't want to, why should they? . . . Why should Portsea be the Cinderella of the City, with its slipper in the mud flats and no-one willing to go in after it? There was indeed a time when the City regarded the district as the particular bright jewel in its crown. That time could come again.[20]

It is perhaps just as well that the Councillor accepted a long-term project for that is surely what seems to be the case. By 1939, 500 old properties had been demolished, some of the people dispossessed being moved to Council estates at Hilsea, and the Unicorn Street/ Orange Street site had still to be opened. The war years would obviously put a stop to development, but in 1973 the *News* drew attention to the 'blueprint for happier days . . . The people of Portsea are sick to death of well-wishers'[21] while nothing was getting done; from a survey taken at the time:

> Litter and refuse accentuate the general air of neglect. . . disrepair and dampness in some homes, overflows from defective ball valves, (all) create considerable nuisance.

In 1980, under the heading 'Golden Blueprint is still waiting', the *News* observes:

> Portseas's golden year was 1978. It was then Councillors turned their attention to Portsmouth's most depressing, unkempt, and neglected area. . .

A 'glossy £3m blueprint' had been drawn up, but still nothing had been done;[22] it might however be no more than just to recall tales of Blossom Alley, White's Row and Godden Court – and be thankful that they at least had disappeared . . .

Local Colour

History books and official documents are all very well when it comes to providing the hard core of a story, but to bring that story to life, to make it real and recognisable, the reader should also listen to the man who was there at the time, born in the district.

Walter Besant was born in August 1836 in St. George's Square, Portsea, the third son of William Besant, a local merchant. He did well at school, obtained a place at Christ's College, Cambridge, and intended to make a career in the Church; but circumstances led him away from this plan, to work for a time in Mauritius, and later to act as Secretary to the Palestine Exploration Fund. At the same time he was producing an enormous number of books, from serious works such as his *Survey on Western Palestine* to the many novels written in partnership with his barrister colleague, James Rice. He was editor of the *Author*, and he was renowned for his work on historical research; it was anticipated that his *Survey of London* would prove a masterpiece, but regrettably he died before the work was completed.

In spite of his many national and international interests he recalled his home town with affection, and it is clear that he knew the Dockyard area intimately:

It must have been when I was a child of six or eight . . . that I saw, for the first time, a man in the stocks. I remember him well, because I was immensely impressed with the shamefulness of it, and I expected to see the prisoner hanging his head and weeping. Not a bit of it. The hardened villain actually sat up, faced the footlights, and grinned merrily all the time.

As a youth he was much impressed by the convict hulks that lay in the harbour, and it seems he felt some sympathy for the men who were brought ashore to work in the Dockyard, for it was his pleasure to lighten their work by secretly passing them a quid of tobacco whenever the opportunity arose:

(The convict) made no sign, he never moved or looked up. He just covered the package with his boot, and continued his work. . . Presently the man straightened himself out: he looked at his tool: he picked up a stone as if to knock off something: he hammered it and looked at it again critically. The warder, who had watched his movement, turned his back, satisfied that it was harmless. In a moment the quid was transferred to the man's mouth. Oh, the rapture of that quid! He could not express his gratitude in words, but with a glance of his eyes he could, and did.[23]

His *Tale of Portsmouth Town*[24] is a beguiling mixture of fact and very typical Victorian fiction, but the pictures he paints of the houses, the people, the Dockyard, and The Hard cannot be bettered.

He described a small four-roomed house close to the Dockyard wall, in Victory Row:

which led out of Nelson Street and was a broad, blind court, bounded on one side and at the end by the Dockyard wall. It was not a dirty and confined court, but quite the reverse, being large and clean, and a very cathedral close for quietness.

This might appear to conflict with the more usual picture of such courts being small and dark and infested, but he was not the only one to comment that poverty did not necessarily mean dirt and squalor.

He went on to relate his memory of the wall that ran the length of the Dockyard perimeter:

. . . built of a warm red brick, (it) had a broad sloping top, on which grew wallflowers, long grasses, and stonecrop; overhanging the wall was a row of great elms, in the branches of which there was a rookery, so that all day long you could listen if you wished to the talk of the rooks . . They have cut down the elms now, and driven the rooks to find other shelter. Very likely in their desire to sweep away everything that is pretty, they have torn the wallflowers and grasses off the wall. And if these are gone, no doubt Victory Row has lost its only charm.

Did Victory Row exist, or is it – like Nelson Street – just an all-embracing piece of the author's imagination?

The hero of his book, the Polish boy Ladislas, could see into the Dockyard from the upper window of the house where he was staying:

> There was the Long Row, where resided the Heads of Departments; the Short Row, in which lived functionaries of lower rank – I believe the two Rows do not know each other in society; there was the great Reservoir, supported on tall and spidery legs . . . there was the Rope Walk, a quarter of a mile long, in which I know walked incessantly up and down the workmen who turned hanks of yarn into strong cables smelling of fresh tar; there were the buildings where other workmen made blocks, bent beams, shaped all the parts of ships; . . . there was a pool of sea water, and sometimes I saw boys paddling up and down in it; and there was always the busy crowd of officers and sailors going up and down, some of them god-like, with cocked hats, epaulettes and swords.

In library records there are frequent references to dishonesty and drunkenness in the area, to the wicked ways of the harlots who beset each sailor as he came ashore – but those records are dry and severely critical; how much more vivid and exciting is a description of the scene along The Hard, as Besant recalled from his childhood:

> It was a long procession, consisting of sailors marching, every man with a lady on his arm, two and two, along the middle of the street, singing as they went. They wore long curls, these jolly tars, shining with grease, hanging down on either side below, or rather in front of, their hats . . . *The Royal Frederick* had been paid off that morning, and a thousand Jack Tars were all together chucking away the money in a few days which it had taken them three years to earn...

Not surprisingly, the procession came to a halt at a public-house, where an old man was playing a jolly tune on his fiddle:

> Dancing then set in, though it was still early in the morning, with great severity. With dancing, drinks. With both, songs...

The Ship Anson and Victoria and Albert, The Hard, 1903.
(PCL. Photograph: D.G. Dine)

There was the tradition that being ashore meant drink as long as the money lasted. It sometimes lasted a week, or even a fortnight, and was sometimes got through in a day or two. There were harpies and pirates in every house which was open to Jack.

This was the picture as Walter Besant saw it in the mid-nineteenth century, but then, with the beginning of the Crimean War there was a change of scene, familiar in any war:

> It was pitiful to see our brave fellows, full of fire and enthusiasm, go down the narrow streets of the town to the Dockyard Gates on their way to the East. They marched in loose order, headed by the Colonel, the bands playing "The Girl I left behind me".

He described 'women crying, some of them even kissing the soldiers; the men waving hats and shouting; the children laughing and running for joy at so splendid a spectacle'.

In an outburst of patriotism that was completely in tune with the times, he talked of:

> The despatch of the great and splendid Black Sea and Baltic Fleets . . . never was so gallant a fleet sent forth from any shore, never were shores more crowded with those who came to criticise and stayed to cheer.

He listed several of the ships, led out to sea by the Queen in her 'steamer', *Fairy*, 'the pretty little yacht with her three sloping masts'.

The months passed, and the war was not over and won quite as quickly as had been anticipated:

> . . . And after a while they began to send the wounded home. To receive them a hospital was built in one of the meadows under the Ramparts . . . in 1856, the sick and wounded were brought home by every ship . . . and week by week, sometimes daily might be seen filing up the long and narrow street a long and dismal procession. It consisted of sailors carrying stretchers, four to every stretcher. There was no band now . . . (and) the townsfolk who had turned out to wave their handkerchiefs when the soldiers left came out now to greet them back. But what a greeting! . . .

If there were grief and sympathy for the wounded, it could however be said that the ill wind of war blew some good in the direction of the local shopkeepers, for 'a man who had a shop near The Hard had but to open it and stand all day taking the sailors' money as fast as they passed it over the counter'.

These are Walter Besant's pictures of Portsea, conjured up in his *Tale of Portsmouth Town*, but there is one more that has a place here, a quick sketch of the public house, the focus of a man's enjoyment and almost his only source of pleasure when his pockets were all but empty:

> . . . from behind the red curtains of a sailors' public-house . . . Listen! It is the sailors' hornpipe . . . (it is) a low room, and it is redolent of a thousand compound smells, ancient, fish-like, capable of knocking a stronger man down and stunning him. . . The windows have never been open for twenty or thirty years. There was rum in it (the smell), plenty of beer, a very large quantity of tobacco, onions, beef-steaks, mutton-chops, boiled pork and cabbage, pea-soup, more tobacco, more rum, more beer.

There were public houses and beer houses, restaurants and 'dining rooms' in almost every street in Portsea; The Hard was reputed to have more beer houses than most, but nonetheless Besant painted a generous picture:

> . . . It was a place which seemed to belong to the previous century. There were no great houses and handsome shops, but in their place a picturesque row of irregular cottages, no two of which were exactly alike, but which resembled each other in certain particulars. They were two-storeyed houses: the upper storey was very low (and) the ground-floor was below the level of the street. . . you had to stoop if you were tall, to get into the doorway, and then . . . you generally fell headlong down a step of a foot or so. Unless the houses were shops they had only one window below and one above, because the tax on windows obliged people to economise their light. The roofs were of red tiles, high-pitched, and generally broken-backed; stone-crop and house-leek grew upon them. The Hard existed then only for the sailors. There were one or two jewellers who bought as well as sold; many public-houses, and a plentiful supply of rascally pay-agents. . . In old times the high tide had washed right up to the foot of these houses . . . But they built a stone wall, which kept back the water and allowed a road to be made protected by an iron railing . . . A wooden bench was placed by the railing near the beach, on which sat every day and all day old sailors in a row. It was their club, their daily rendezvous, the place where they discussed old battles, smoked pipes and lamented bygone days. . .

Dockyard Main Gate, 1905.
(PCL. Photograph: D.G. Dine)

H.M.S. Dreadnought. Launched by Kind Edward VII, 10 February 1905
(Portsmouth Royal Dockyard Historical Society)

PART II

'WHAT DOES A MAN NEED TO EARN?'

Until recent years the Dockyard was the chief source of employ-ment, for skilled artisans, labourers and apprentices alike, and it is these men and their families who made up the main body of population in Portsea. Indeed, it was they who had first moved out of the grossly overcrowded Portsmouth Town to settle near the Dockyard, where the area known as Portsea Common was developed in 1792 to become the present-day Portsea.

At its peak, in 1813, the labour force in the Dockyard numbered some 3,580, but the years after the Napoleonic Wars had seen massive redun-dancy, together with wage cuts for those still in work. The situation continued to deteriorate, until in 1830 (the worst year on record) only 1,610 remained on the Dockyard books.[1]

The fact that there were so many unemployed contributed in no small measure to the depression and downgrading of the area they lived in, Portsea and its immediate neighbours Landport and Kingston. Even the labouring jobs were denied to these men, for convicts had been put to work in the yard, adding considerably to the bitterness and unrest that existed at the time.[2]

With the development of steam, there was some improvement in conditions and by 1841 there was work for more than 2,000 men; over a five-year period four docks, a steam basin and an assortment of other buildings were constructed, much of it by convict labour. Indeed, the project was considered to be of such significance that Queen Victoria was invited to attend at the opening on 25 May 1848.

This was an occasion for much rejoicing on the part of the local population, not only because a visit from royalty was invariably counted an occasion for a show of loyalty and enthusiasm – but also because further extension to the Dockyard would surely mean a greater number of men employed. It was reported that, to celebrate the occa-sion there was the 'agreeable spectacle (of) 2186 men of the Dockyard Battalion and 1050 of Mr. Rolls workmen being regaled with English fare and plenty of beer'.

The year before, the area known as New Buildings in Portsea had been acquired by the Admiralty, extending the Dockyard still further until by the end of the century, it would have covered an area of some 300 acres, with accommodation that justified its claim to being the country's leading seaport. Such development meant that for a time at least Dockyard workers were in demand once again; but this happy state of affairs was to last only a short while, until in 1849 the Admiralty called for a reduction in expenditure and once again the work force was reduced, leaving only 3,500 shipwrights and a corresponding number in other relevant trades.

Throughout the years that followed a wide-ranging reduction in Dockyard personnel resulted in massive unemployment, and this could only be alleviated by a national scheme of emigration to Canada; thus, many Portsmouth families found themselves joined by others from as far as Chatham and Woolwich, embarking in Indian troopships deployed to take them on their long journey – 391 men, women and children sailed in the *Crocodile* in April 1869, another 776 in the *Serapis* on 1 May, and a year later, in June 1870, the *Crocodile* took a third batch of emigrants to Canada. Most of them settled in happily and did well in their new homes, so much so that 'letters were soon pouring back to Portsmouth often with the addendum that the writers never wanted to set eyes on the place again'.[3] But for those left behind it was a question of seeking out work of some sort, on projects purposely put in train, like the construction of the sea wall to the east of Southsea Castle. For carpenters and joiners at least there was regular employment available in the building trade as development spread rapidly in the areas of Kingston, Landport and Southsea.

Queen Victoria's Golden Jubilee in 1887 should by rights have been a time for great celebration, and indeed the town made every effort to join in with the gala mood. But at this same period another thousand men, mostly shipwrights, were discharged from the Dockyard and the Jubilee festivities were overshadowed by public indignation, for this was the heaviest blow to employment since 1869, and over the next two years another 850 people left the country, this time to go to South America. For many it was an unfortunate decision:

> This scheme was not Admiralty-sponsored; it was conceived by a shrewd Argentine Government needing man-power, and needing it quickly. The only lavish gesture was represented by the magnificent brochures which lured the sacked Dockyards mateys to sign on the dotted line in the grubby office the moguls of Buenos Aires had rented in Broad Street. . . On arrival at Buenos Aires the Portsmouth multitude was marched to the "Immigrants' Home". This they found to be crowded out already with Italians, who were the most-

favoured race among the migrants, being accustomed to
accept bare subsistence living conditions.[4]

Rats attacked the children as they slept, resulting in the death of five
babies; while the men battled to protect their children at night, by day
they were set to hewing massive blocks of stone to build the new
Government buildings. For this they they were paid 2s. a day, a sum that
was quite inadequate to support a family, and disenchanted, several of
them gave up and returned to this country.

At the turn of the century there had been little or no improvement in
the situation, and at one stage it was announced that the Admiralty was
proposing yet another batch of dismissals. But this time public protest
caused such an uproar that it was finally agreed there would no mass
dismissal, the men being permitted to go a few at a time, so that
hardship would not be felt as severely as it had in the past.

With the coming of war there had been an urgent need to step up the
production of shipping, and by 1918 the Dockyard work force had been
increased out of all recognition, more than 23,000 men working day and
night shifts between them. This gave the men a new sense of their true
worth, and – no doubt aware that the Armistice would bring with it the
old and familiar redundancy – they negotiated with the Admiralty for
some security for the future. They did away with the old custom of
Admiralty officials meeting employees' representatives to discuss problems, replacing this with Shop Committees, established 'for the
purpose of discussing and obtaining a settlement or understanding of
matters regarding welfare and conditions of service'.

As far as it went, this was a great success, but it it could not prevent
what was described as the 'Price of Peace'. The fact that redundancies
were once again spread over a period did go some way to alleviating the
position, with Admiral Jackie Fisher working hard to bring some sta-
bility to the employment situation. Nevertheless 1917 was to be the last
year that capital ships were built in Portsmouth Dockyard. In 1919 the
men felt driven to some positive action, eventually banding together to
present a petition to the Prince of Wales demanding work for the
unemployed.

A year later the Admiralty ordered the building of a 10,000 ton ship
for commercial use, and this went some way to producing work, but
although it seemed a successful venture for some reason it was never
repeated. Uncertainty persisted, with four hundred men put on short
time as a result of the tramways losing money; others were put to work
extending the Esplanade and later to the building of the Western Road
in Paulsgrove. The Clan Line agreed to send its steamers to Portsmouth
for refitting, though this work was to end within twelve months, leaving
1,000 back on the streets while those still lucky enough to be in work
were invited to accept a reduction of hours.

Address 24 Gloucester St - Portsea

Buddery, Cyril Entered Bermuda Yard as apprentice April 21st 1903 Date of Birth 3-10-1888. Transferred to Portsmouth June 1906. Entered as Coppersmith Ap. 21st 1909 Discharged at own request Jan 1911. Entered M C D Portsmouth Yard May 1911. Discharged on Reduction Sept 1911. Entered Devonport Yard Sept 1911 Transferred to Reliance August 1915 Returned to ~~England and Transferred to~~ Devonport July 1918 Transferred to Portsmouth Feb 19- 1919 Rate of pay 40/- ~~Transferred to~~ Bermuda July 31st 1919

Address 9 British Street Portsea

Palmer. William Samuel Entered Yard as Labourer Rat 21-11-16 Date of Birth 2-5-68. @ 24/- per week + 7/- Warbonus (Vice Summers) Made Skilled Lab 17-12-17 + increased to 26/- Discharged on Reduction 9-4-20

Address 25 Little Britain St Portsea

Clark. Rose. entered as Womanworker 12-11-17 @ 26/6 per week (including W.B.) Date of Birth 15:8:77. Increased to ~~38/~~ Increased to 34/- 15-7-18 Increased to 39/- 1-9-18 Discharged on Reduction 14-3-19.

'Discharged on reduction', 1911, 1919 and 1920
(Portsmouth Royal Dockyard Historical Society)

The Council voted £25,000 for establishing a variety of work schemes for the relief of hardship in the town. The Goodwill Fund was reopened, with £14,000 being raised by the end of the year to help the 7,000 now unemployed. But by 1924 it was recognised that, for workers in the Dockyard, matters could hardly get worse when it was decided that the Fleet be reduced from some fifty-five battle ships to only ten.

The 'All-In' contributory insurance scheme was one of the few good things to come out of those hard times, originating in the Dockyard in the mid-twenties and spreading through the town to workshops and business enterprises. Not surprisingly, it was restricted to the working classes, and it proved a great source of comfort to the fortunate ones actually in work, for a contribution of 2d. a week included all members of a man's family. Ten years after the scheme had been set up, the Dockyard alone was able to hand on £5,000 per annum to two of the City's hospitals.

The Portsmouth Gas Company had instituted a pension scheme for its employees, and the Corporation followed suit in 1924. But such action could not dispel what was a national discontent, resulting in the General Strike of 1926, and there were hard years ahead for everyone. Almost the only glimmer of cheer came in 1930 when the Admiralty, 'moving with the spirit of the times' instituted the practice of a week's holiday-with-pay, a bonus extended to all their employees.

As for the women, during the 1850s they had begun to take a positive place in the employment market. With so many local men away at sea or serving abroad, there were many wives and widows living alone, often with large families and with little or no financial support; however, throughout the second half of the nineteenth century, they were beginning to explore ways of augmenting their income, initially taking up the opportunities offered by an unexpected demand for domestic servants in the new and comparatively well-off area of Southsea.

There was an alternative to domestic service, provided by the growing need for dressmakers, shirtmakers and, in particular, staymakers. The managers of these industries encouraged the employment of 'outworkers' since it meant a saving on factory space, while for the women themselves it meant they could stay home to mind the children while they worked. They were cheap labour and in plentiful supply, many of them without any other means of support; cashing in on this happy combination of circumstances, the Portsmouth workshops were soon to become the major centre for the corset industry.

There was a noticeable percentage of women who described themselves as of 'independent means' and since they far outnumbered those in either the clothing industry or domestic service, the conclusion may be drawn that they were probably following the 'oldest profession'.[5] Certainly the darker alleys of Portsea abounded with prostitutes, and

Shipwrights, Portsmouth Dockyard, c.1912

Jetty Party "All Merry and Bright", 1912
(Portsmouth Royal Dockyard Historical Society)

the constant presence of a large number of young men stationed in and around the Dockyard area would account for the proliferation of brothels, so vehemently condemned by the worthy Father Dolling. It was thanks to his efforts that the majority – the hard core of 'bad houses' centred on Landport and Portsea – began to disappear, and it may not be pure coincidence that it was also during this time, the latter half of the century, that with the eradication of the brothels the number of illegitimate births was reduced quite considerably.

In the nineteenth century the employment of children was probably no more reprehensible in Portsmouth than elsewhere in the country. The poor accepted that there was little help to be had from the authorities and therefore, using all resources available, children were expected to work for long hours from a very early age.

There is a graphic description of conditions in a Portsmouth factory producing ladies' corsets:

> Here twelve or thirteen hours a day were normally worked, and extended in the summer months to sixteen hours. These stay factories were considered by some to be places of temptation and vice, and as early as 1838 the excessive drinking in which young stay-workers indulged was commented upon in the *Hampshire Telegraph*. Cutting out the stiff and heavy lining made the children's fingers ache, and only one firm, Helby's in Portsea, provided stools for the girls to sit on.[6]

It was considered perfectly acceptable that the hundreds of women employed as outworkers should be helped at home by young children of eight and nine, who were put to work on the simpler tasks of hemming and stitching, or threading the long cotton laces into ladies' corsets.

For the older girls, particularly those from the Workhouse, domestic service appears to have been the only means of employment, to the extent that, while still at elementary school they were actually prepared for this work. While this meant they would be assured of a roof over their heads many of them were to endure long hours and harsh treatment with little hope of escape, should they be so foolish as to leave their place of employment without a reference, to go in search of more congenial work .

The boys had the choice of two very reasonable careers, either going to sea or working in the Dockyard. Those who served two years at sea could look forward to the chance of an apprenticeship, serving only five years instead of the usual seven. Naval apprentices were required to remain in the Service until they were twenty-eight, and though the life was hard once they were at sea, the pay was fair and they had the satisfaction of a guaranteed three meals a day.

VOLLER'S "Hercules" Corset

FITTED WITH ==========
"HERCULES" UNBREAKABLE STEELS.

"Hercules"
Steels
give to
every
Movement
of the
Body.

Support
without
Pressure.

♦ ♦

Sample.
Steel
Post Free.

STOCK NUMBERS—

Qual. I	Dove only. 13½-in. Double Busk	2/3
„ 2	Dove, Curved Hip, 12½ in. Straight Front Suspenders	3/6
„ 3	Dove only, 13½-in. „ No Suspenders	4/6
„ 4	{ Dove, White 14-in. Heavy Straight „ { Sky and White, Sky and Black—very durable. Stock Sizes in each Quality, 19 to 30.	5/6

Made to Order in various Materials, 1/6 Extra.

The following Stock Numbers can usually be Sent
by Return.

Spoon Busk Corsets

Model A.
Dove. Boned Whalebone, 12½-in. Spoon   **3/6**
Stock Sizes 19—30

Model B.
Dove or Black, Boned Whalebone, 13½-in. Spoon **3/6**
Stock Sizes 19—30

Model C.
Dove Boned Whalebone. 13½-in Triple Spoon.
Hand Fanned Pink. Stock Sizes 19—26   **4/6**

Long Waisted Straight Busk Corsets.

Model 145.
Dove or Dark Grey, deep over hips and back,
well supported by Side Steels. 12½-in Busk.
Front Suspenders. Stock Sizes 19—30   **2/6**

Model 146.
Putty only. Long Waisted, all Side Steels.
15 in. Busk. Stock Sizes 19—26   **3/-**

Model 147.
Dove only. 14½-in. Heavy Busk.
Stock Sizes 19—28   **3/9**

Model 148.
Drab Jean. 14-in. Heavy Busk.
Boned Whalebone   **5/6**

Model 149.
Dark Grey Coutil, Boned Whalebone.
Hand Fanned, Cardinal   **6/-**

Mail Order Department

The large number of unsolicited testimonials
received from all parts of the United Kingdom
is a proof of the all round excellence of
the goods

Corsets Accurately Copied to Customers own Patterns
: : Moderate Charges. : :
Estimate with a selection of Materials, Post Free.

Remittance must accompany all orders.
Cash refunded in full if not satisfactory.

IMPORTANT.

Cheques and Postal Orders should be made payable to MADAME
VOLLER and crossed National Provincial Bank Landport.

Please fill in and retain Counterfoil of Postal Orders.

Any article in this Catalogue sent Carriage Paid in the
United Kingdom and Channel Islands.

Foreign Postage Extra.

Madame Voller's Mail Order Corset Business in Kingston Road: Extract from Catalogue,
c. 1913.
(PCRO 1009A)

Dockyard apprentices worked under skilled craftsmen and emerged armed with a useful trade at the end of their time, but this did not apply to all the boys working in the Dockyard. Some of them, no more than nine or ten years old, would be required to work a twelve-hour day in the rope shop or cleaning bilges and boilers.

It has been claimed that at least until 1911 one in every two men in Portsmouth was employed in the Dockyard; but it could in fact be said that most Portsea and Landport men were working for the Admiralty in one way or another, if only as suppliers of food, drink and clothing.

But it was not only in the Dockyard that people found life hard and terms of employment unattractive, for though they might consider themselves fortunate to be working at all, shop assistants had been rebelling for years against conditions at work, in particular the excessively long hours of business. In some desperation a public meeting was called to petition for a reduction in working hours and as a result it was recommended that shops be closed on Sundays, and that weekeday closing time should be 9.00 p.m. in Summer and 8.00 p.m. in Winter – except for Saturdays when shops would remain open until 10.00 p.m. all year round.

For a time it seemed that the proposal had foundered for it was not until three years later, in 1846, that the Association which had been formed specifically to achieve more acceptable hours of business, succeeded in giving notice of a six-month trial period during which closing time would be 8.00 p.m.

There were many fine shops in Queen Street, the main thoroughfare through Portsea, but in the early 1900s many of the side streets were just as busy. Joseph Daufman, a Queen Street tailor and outfitter, observed that 'Portsea was a world of its own between the first and second world wars. In Queen Street you could buy everything from a pin to an elephant'[7], and as well as the usual butchers, grocers and fishmongers, there was just about every trade imaginable.

Daufman himself was born in Portsea in rooms over his father's naval outfitter's premises, a business which had opened on the west side of Queen Street and moved opposite in 1914 where in due course Joseph and his brother Harold took over from their father. The family name was still represented in the 1930s, when Isaac Daufman ran one of the many cafés in Queen Street.

There were several naval outfitters and tailors – almost as many as there were beer retailers, for these were everywhere. In 1903 there were four in Unicorn street, five in North Street and many more beside. In Union Street there were two dressmakers, and at No. 66 Miss Elizabeth Hinds ran a day school, but thirty years later the school had gone. So too had the charmingly named *Heart in Hand*, a public house sadly to be rechristened the *Portsea Arms*; George Ayles, a tailor at 11 Union Street

The Premises of Messrs. William Treadgold in Bishop Street.
(City Secretariat, Portsmouth)

'… in Queen Street you could buy everything…'
(Portsmouth Royal Dockyard Historical Society)

was still there thirty years on, the fascia board now reading 'and Son', and Walter Bolitho was still a solicitor at No.40.

Another public house, with an equally diverting name, the *Hat in Hand* at No.1 Camden Buildings had, by 1931, become simply *The Camden*. No doubt the *Hat in Hand* seemed a curious name for the place, once Mrs. Sarah Ann Tayler at No.3 had taken down the sign proclaiming she was a 'hatter'. Now she was gone, to be replaced by the more prosaic 'Camden Engineering Co., Motor Engineers'.

Cross Street had its butcher, its plumber, two 'coal and wood dealers', a fishmonger and a 'whitesmith'. In Butcher Street there were three bootmakers, Andrew King, a brass founder at No.30, and Miss Sarah Freemantle, a 'starcher' , while in Victory Road there had once been Frederick Avery, a sea chest maker. By 1931 Victory Road and Unicorn Road had become almost entirely residential, and while four of the five beer retailers in Butcher Street remained, by the start of the war in 1939 there was only one.[8]

Aside from these small and mostly individual enterprises, there were the larger, long-standing businesses employing several local men, such as William Treadgold and Co. Ltd., iron and steel merchants. Established in Bishop Street toward the end of the eighteenth century, the Company continued to function as a family concern until after World War Two, their interests extending far beyond iron and steel to take in such projects as the development of the Portsmouth Harbour Pier Company and involvement in several land transactions.

The range of goods supplied by the firm seems limitless, 'everything from Arnotts Ventilators (10s. 6d.) to zinc baths (9s. 6d.)', and a black-smith's shop on the premises not only took on every kind of repair service from shoeing horses to providing spare parts for lawn mowers, but had the capacity to manufacture the huge steel girders required for the Theatre Royal. Among their clients they included several large building contractors, together with the Hospital, the Portsea Gas Company and Portsea Pier, not forgetting such one-man businesses as undertakers (for whom Treadgold's manufactured coffin handles), bricklayers and even an egg merchant. Occasionally the Dockyard sent in for supplies but, surprisingly, these were only for small and individual items rather than the full-scale contract jobs that might reasonably have been reserved for a local trader.

The company resisted the growing popularity of motorised transport, insisting on horse-power because, it was said, it would not look good to have a motor vehicle stopping outside a smithy! Consequently, steel imported through the Camber dock was taken by horse-drawn trailer to Treadgold's, and it was the custom when work was finished for the men to be given a token for one pint of best beer at the *Curzon Howe* public house.[9]

One of the bigger employers of women living in Portsea was the firm of Chilcot and Williams, originating in about 1847, when James Chilcot set up in business as a staymaker in nearby Surrey Street. He went into partnership with Thomas Williams in 1869 and the firm remained a family concern until just before the start of the last war.

While Queen Street and the immediate area around was bustling with industry, Lion Terrace remained mainly residential, combined with a variety of individual undertakings; in the early 1900's the Royal Engineers' Office and Mill Dam Barracks were to be found there, so too was the Royal Naval Engineers' Club. Henry Zeffert conducted a cap manufacturing business in the Terrace, there were two 'travelling drapers' and the Portsmouth Trade Protection Society at No.21, and a physician and surgeon. Six ladies ran apartment houses, and Miss Elizabeth Ann Wills and Miss Mary Field ran the 'Ladies School' at No.37. Change came to the Terrace over the years, No.37 becoming 'Levy and Co. Admiralty Contractors', the cap manufacturer replaced by an insurance agent, and the R.N. Engineers' Club at No.12 had gone to Mrs. Emily Brace, who ran the premises as a temperance hotel.

Queen Street had probably seen more change in the early years of the twentieth century than at any other time. For the less fortunate there was now a Ministry of Labour Employment Exchange and at No.142 'George Williams, Refreshment Rooms' had become the *Curzon Howe* public house, appropriately sited on one side of the entrance to St. John's Church, while on the other was the Norfolk Arms. At No.88 'The Sailors' Welcome' had at one time been managed by Robert G. Pither with the assistance of ' Miss Robinson, the Lady Superintendent', but by the Thirties *The Sailors' Welcome* had gone, and in its place stood the restaurant of Joseph Azzopardi. The Jewish Synagogue remained between Nos.53 and 56, and further up the road Samuel Harris and Son conducted their business, a 'mourning warehouse'. Perhaps the greatest innovation of all would have been the building and grand opening of the Queen's Cinema, that sign of the times so soon to fall into disrepair and eventual demolition.

In the years leading up to the 1914-18 war, Corporation workmen had been promised a minimum wage of 24s. a week, but by comparison a labourer's wage at that time was seldom more than 20s. per week, from which he might have to pay as much as 5s. to 6s. in rent.

The true extent of such poverty is illustrated in a book by Maud Pember Reeves, first published in 1913:[10]

> How does a working man's wife bring up a family on 20s. a week? Assuming that there are four children, and that it costs 4s. a week to feed a child, there would be but 4s. left on which to feed both parents, and nothing at all for coal, gas, clothes, insurance, soap, or rent. Four shillings is the amount allowed the foster-mother for food in the case of a child boarded out

by some Boards of Guardians . . .

As if this were not bad enough, the question of housing was an added problem:

> . . . decent housing has as much influence on children's health as, given a certain minimum, the quality and quantity of their food. That is to say, it is as important for a young child to have light, air, warmth, and freedom from damp, as it is for it to have sufficient and proper food.... Rents of less than 6s. a week are generally danger-signals, unless the amount is for a single room. Two rooms for 5s. 6d. are likely to be basement rooms or very small ground-floor rooms, through one of which, perhaps, all the other people in the house have to pass. . . The airlessness of basement dwellings is much enhanced by the police regulations, which insist on shut windows at night on account of the danger of burglary!. . . Four and six paid for two rooms meant two tiny rooms below the level of the alley-way outside. . .

It was suggested that tenants might have been able to do better for themselves if they knew their rights:

> They put up with broken and defective grates which burn twice the coal for half the heat; they accept plagues of rats or of vermin as acts of God; they deplore a stopped-up drain without making an effective complaint, because they are afraid of being told to find new quarters if they make too much fuss. . .

There was never enough room; children had to share two and three to a bed, and still the babies continued to arrive. Such birth control as became available was organised by groups of well-intentioned middle class women who had plenty of sympathy but little hope of success, for in most cases birth control was the subject of mistrust on the part of the menfolk, even if their wives would have welcomed the prospect....

When it came to feeding the family, priority was invariably given to the wage earner, the best going to him, the next best to the children, their mother making do on what was left.

For the labourer on 20s. a week, there was little to eat beyond potatoes, bread and a small quantity of meat, fish and cheese. When potatoes were in short supply there might be suet pudding instead; fresh milk seldom came to the table, for it was too expensive at 4d. a quart and tinned milk, quite unsuitable for small children, might on occasions be substituted. If there were bacon, it went to the man of the house; tea, butter, jam and fresh vegetables came in such small quantities as to make little or no difference to the value of the meal:

> The diet where there are several children is obviously chosen for its cheapness, and is of the filling, stodgy kind. There is not enough of anything but bread. There is no variety. Nothing is considered but money.

Between the two World Wars food prices remained remarkably unchanged. In 1914 a pound of thin flank of beef could be purchased for 6½d., less for frozen, while breast of lamb was available at 4d. per pound; by 1938 these prices had increased in most cases by as little as one penny. A seven pound bag of flour might be threepence dearer in 1938 and a 4 lb. loaf of bread had gone up by fourpence to 9d. For the few who could afford butter there was little change in price during this same period, and margarine had actually gone down by ½d. tp 6½d.

Many people had taken on allotments during the war and they kept them going afterwards, to supply their families with such basic needs as potatoes, for these had been in short supply during the war, the price going up from 4d. to 1s. 2d. a pound by 1920. But while the price of foodstuff in general increased only slightly during the 1920s, there were several wage cuts for the lower paid, and it was not until 1930 onward that some sort of balance was reached.

What did a man need to earn to provide adequate food at this time? In 1914 a shipwright would take home a little over 41s., a figure which increased to more than 60s. in 1930 and 68s. some years later; bricklayers, carpenters and plumbers were all paid much the same, 39s. to 40s. a week, increasing in the following ten years in an upward curve common to several other trades, to 73s. in 1924. This however was to be reduced by as much as 8s. in 1933-34, only to rise again in 1938 to about 73s.[11]

As to the hours of work, in the mid-nineteenth century the bricklayer had been working as much as 58 hours a week but by the early 1900s this had been reduced to fifty, and by 1920 to forty-four hours, a figure that was to remain constant until 1965.

There were quite startling discrepancies between wages for men and those for women. For instance, a man working in a laundry in the 1920s might earn 48s. for a 44½-hour week, whereas his wife would be paid only 26s.. They, too, had suffered a cut in the early 1930s, but the discrepancy remained, and it appears common to most trades – the woman earning little more than half that of the man. In 1935 little had changed – a man working in one of the public utility services could earn just under 58s. a week, a woman 28s., while a girl under eighteen might be paid 15s. 6d., but a youth in the same age bracket would take home very nearly 26s..

By 1928 there had been some recovery from the desperate shortage of work which had led to the General Strike, and in order to maintain and improve this situation locally the Council went to considerable lengths to introduce new industry into the City.

Several proposals were put forward to induce manufacturers to set up business in the locality. For instance they might be offered sites at a nominal rent, electric power could be provided at special rates, and the payment of general rates might be waived. But a Special Committee set up to investigate these ideas rejected them one by one, on the grounds that 'a Municipal Authority has no power to grant preference to particular persons or bodies in the matter of rates, electric light, or the like'.

Not that the Committee was against the influx of new industry; it was simply a question of the right to take such action, and on a more positive note it was suggested that a register of suitable factory sites be compiled and circulated to interested parties. The Electric Light Committee might be approached with a view to negotiating a reduction in charges, while the Railway Companies could be encouraged to improve their goods services from Portsmouth to the Midlands and the North of England. The Committee even cast its eyes over Langstone Harbour, suggesting that this might be converted to a commercial port, but though this idea was tabled more than once, it was never found to be practicable.[12]

The Council has on occasions been accused of a lack of foresight when it comes to the reinvestment of profit, but in spite of this and a continuing need for economy, during the mid-twenties the trade situation did begin to look brighter. There was some road improvement in the City – though it was 1937 before the long-awaited Eastern Way was completed – and with the opening of the Airport in 1932, people were conscious that the City was making a fresh and more positive drive toward prosperity. Southsea's holiday industry provided work for many in guest houses and in sea-front enterprises; there were more than 8,000 people employed in transport in the City, and building, timber-importing, brickmaking, glassmaking and the electricity and gas services all contributed to a growing sense of security. They were even boring for oil under Portsdown Hill . . .[13]

PART III

WHAT OF THE CHILDREN?

In an area where the houses were damp and dark and hemmed in upon each other, where sewage ran freely in the alleys, frequently flooding into cellars, where prostitution and drunkenness were commonplace – what was to become of the children?

The description of Messum's Court[1] could well apply to many of the courts and alleys in 19th century Portsea – the notorious Blossom Alley, The Dell, White's Row – most of them a stone's throw from the wider and more affluent Queen Street. And it was in this dank maze of streets, some less than three feet wide, that the children had to exist as best they could. Mortality was high, over 8% of children under five dying in their first year. Proper food was almost unknown, cooking facilities were primitive and invariably unclean, and sanitation dependent upon an erratic water supply..

The health of the young was further jeopardised by inadequate clothing, resulting in many of them succumbing to bronchial and rheumatic ailments; add to these the illnesses traditionally associated with childhood (whooping cough, measles, sometimes even scarlet fever) against which the child of the poor had little or no resistance, and it is small wonder that so many failed to survive.[2]

In 1850, in an effort to improve the environment, the ratepayers of All Saints, St. Mary and St. Paul combined to send a petition to Mr. Robert Rawlinson, the Superintendent of the General Board of Health inviting him to report on the existing conditions. His findings could hardly have come as a surprise:[3]

> 1. The Borough is not so healthy as it may be, on account of ill-paved and uncleaned streets, imperfect privy accommodation, crowded courts and houses, with large exposed middens and cess-pools. . .
> 2. Excess of disease has been distinctly traced to the undrained and crowded districts, to deficient ventilation, to the

absence of a full water supply, and of sewers and drains generally.

3. The condition of the inhabitants would be improved, their comforts increased and the rates reduced:

(a) By a perfect system of street, court, yard and house drainage.

(b) By a constant and cheap supply of pure water under pressure, laid on to every house and yard, to the entire superseding of all local wells and pumps . . .

(c) By the substitution of water-closets or soilpan apparatus for the more expensive and noxious privies and cesspools which exist, and by a regular and systematic removal of all refuse at short intervals.

(d) By properly paved courts and passages, slaughter-houses, footpaths and surface channels in the borough and by maintaining good roads throughout the district.

He pointed out that all of these improvements could be undertaken under the Public Health Act, and suggested that the Council act upon the Report without delay.

These 'ill-paved and unclean' streets were swarming with the children of the poor, for there was nowhere else for them to play, and in consequence accidents were frequent, the games they played rowdy and unruly. In many cases, parents appeared to feel little or no sense of reponsibility toward their offspring, allowing them to roam free to look after themseslves, and it was a common sight to see small children wandering the streets penniless. They knew little or nothing of schooling, had frequently to sleep rough, and were willing targets for vice and crime.

What might have been considered an improvement in the state of affairs – the drop in illegitimate births in the mid-1800s – was regarded with some concern, there being more than a suspicion that the figures concealed the death of a number of babies, and not always from natural causes:

It was not uncommon for bundles to be fished out of the moat or ditches, or even found at the bottom of respectable gardens, and then discovered to contain infant bodies. . . Such discoveries of babies dead or alive . . . were probably outnumbered by those that went undiscovered, for doubtless the ditches, dung-heaps and the filthy waters of the moat concealed many more pitiful little corpses.[4]

Legitimate or not, those who survived would frequently be taken to Court for quite trivial offences, to be committed to a period in jail

PORTSMOUTH.. — *Royal Seamen and Marines' Orphans Schools.* LL.

The Royal Seamen and Marines' Orphans Schools.
(PCL. Photograph: D.G. Dine)

The Beneficial School, Portsea.
(City Secretariat, Portsmouth)

among hardened criminals. Not surprisingly, they soon developed permanent criminal tendencies themselves, and the setting up of the Reform School in 1854 would prove to be of considerable benefit to the young, harsh and unforgiving though the routine undoubtedly was.

In such living conditions many of the girls were driven to prostitution, some as young as thirteen and fourteen; for them there was no education, no prospect of a better life and little hope of salvation beyond the Female Penitentiary, where those who genuinely wanted to mend their ways could learn the elements of a useful trade.

The eighteenth century had seen the awakening of public conscience over the plight of the underprivileged, and the Charity School was one of the more obvious ways of giving expression to this concern, the idea being that:

> . . . instruction in Bible, and catechism during the formative years of childhood, would build up a God-fearing population, and, at the same time inoculate the children against the habits of sloth, debauchery and beggary, which characterised the lower orders of Society.[5]

The Society for Promoting Christian Knowledge (SPCK) probably did more than any other organisation to encourage the foundation of such schools, while the Beneficial Society, quick to act upon this same theory, created the first of the Charity Schools (later to become known as the Free School for Boys).

There was the Royal Seamen and Marines Orphan Home in St. George's Square, which opened in 1834 with twenty-seven children. Within ten years there were 312 children in attendance, and the Home was obliged to move to Lion Terrace and again to St. Michaels Road some years later. It was founded as a home for orphan girls, while the boys attended daily; they were fed and clothed and given a sound, if basic, education, and the Home continued to thrive until the introduction of the 1894 Education Act when the School was closed to the boys.

There was, too, the Seamen, Marines' and Fishermen's School in Ordnance Row, and the Union Schools, founded in 1846, which went some way toward educating the child inmates, though mostly in terms of providing semi-skilled training for a trade. The Sunday Schools were popular with employers because those children supposedly fortunate enough to be in work could attend without loss of work time; and there were the 'Dame' schools, of questionable value, the women who ran them being little more than child-minders.

At the other end of the scale the Royal Naval Academy provided education for potential midshipmen, and there was Portsmouth Grammar School, founded in 1732, but both of these were virtually unattainable to the poor at that time. In the Portsea area there were several private schools, most of them 'crammers' for the Dockyard apprenticeships. Many of these , like the two below, would advertise their wares in the *Hampshire Telegraph*:

> Girls School, 47 Prince George's St., The Misses Smith teach Grammar, History, Geography, Writing, Cyphering, French, useful and ornamental needlework, £1 per quarter. Music and drawing £1 per quarter extra, 2 vacations of 1 month, Midsummer and Xmas. School is from 9 to 3.

> Portsea Diocese Commercial and Classical School
> Under the Diocesan Board of Education, Queen St., Portsea opposite Lion Gate.
> Principal Jeremiah Andrewes
> Late Mathematical Asst Master of the Royal Academy Gosport
> This establishment has been established for the purpose of offering at a moderate expense, the advantages of a sound education, based on the principles of the Church of England. The general course of instruction will embrace:
> 1. Instruction in the doctrines and duties of Christianity according to the formularies of the Church of England
> 2. English taught grammatically
> 3. Writing.[6]

But perhaps for the children of the poor there would have been little if any schooling, had it not been for the shoemaker, John Pounds.

John Pounds

It might seem that the story of John Pounds[7] has no place in this book, for he died in 1839 at the age of seventy-three, but the foundation of his Ragged School was to have a lasting and vital effect on education, not only in the slum districts of Portsmouth but throughout the country, and the picture would be incomplete without some mention of him and his achievements.

His father was a carpenter in the Dockyard, and it followed that John, leaving school at twelve, should be apprenticed to a shipwright. But only three years later a serious accident left him crippled for life and he had to look elsewhere for a living.

He became a bootmaker, working from the small wooden shop in St. Mary's Street, where he took on the repair of boots and shoes belonging to the poor among his neighbours.

His role as schoolmaster began when he turned his attention to the education of his nephew, Johnnie. The boy was a cripple like himself,

The 'Original Home & Workshop' of John Pounds.
(Portsmouth Polytechnic Central Photography Unit)

spending long hours on his own, and for this reason the neighbours' children were encouraged to come to the workshop to keep Johnnie company. Then, while he still got on with his work, John Pounds began to give more of his time to the children, teaching them to read, to learn passages from the Bible, even to master some degree of Arithmetic.

He discovered he had a flair for teaching, and soon more and more sought to place their children with him; but his little school was for the children of those without money and parents who could pay were told to go elsewhere:

> His was a 'ragged school'. The only pupils to pass the door-way into this seat of learning were those who had dirty faces when they came, and whose poor rags of clothing hung in tattered shreds around their emaciated little bodies.

Apart from the 'Three R's', John Pounds found time to teach them to cook, to mend their clothes, even to mend their boots and shoes, and to help them to be useful with their hands he taught them to make all kinds of wooden toys. He believed it was a positive advantage for everyone to get out into the countryside, not only to enjoy but to observe and to learn, and many times he took his group of children up on to Portsdown Hill; and when it was time to go back into town,the outing invariably ended with a prayer of thanks or a passage from the Bible.

John Pounds was a teacher for twenty years, rewarded by seeing his pupils go into the world with some chance of making a success of their lives. Many joined the Army and the Navy, and seeing what could be done with so few resources, the well-to-do of the town acknowledged that they too had a duty to the less fortunate; before long other schools were being opened, run on the lines of John Pounds', and toward the end of the century funds were raised to open a new and somewhat different venture, The John Pounds' Home. This was a Training Institution for twenty of the older girls, where they were prepared for domestic service and subsequently found suitable places of employment.[8]

It follows that as the accepted Founder of Ragged Schools, John Pounds was ultimately responsible for the Ragged School Movement, which began in London, supported by people with money and influence – until Lord Shaftesbury stepped into the limelight, becoming in 1844 the first President of the Ragged School Union, or The Shaftesbury Society and Ragged Schools Union, as it became known.

The Union grew in strength throughout the British Isles, establishing as many as fifty Mission centres and several Holiday Homes, run exclusively for the benefit of children who would otherwise have little chance of getting away to the sea and countryside. This love of the country was a basic facet of John Pounds' character, and the Union never lost sight of the work he had begun, caring particularly for crippled children, setting up the Free Dinners scheme, and as a regular treat, seeing to it that hundreds of poor chilldren were provided with a Christmas Dinner, just as their founder had done. With the introduction of the Elementary School, there was no longer any need to make special provision for the poor, but the Union survived to continue in its aim to be a strong influence for the wellbeing of children worldwide . . .

The 'Old Benny'

The Portsea Beneficial Society looked beyond the aims of the the Society's founder a hundred years before, by undertaking not only its members insurance against sickness, unemployment and death, but also the education of orphans and children of the poor.

The Beneficial School was housed in a fine-looking two-storey building in Old Rope Walk, Portsea, the ground floor given over to two rooms, one for boys and one for girls, with the members' meeting room above. But according to Dr. Henry Slight's report on conditions in the school, the facilities left much to be desired:

> The rooms are ventilated by six windows at the side, and one large one at the end; but being closely surrounded by buildings they are dark and close. Average scholars 240 boys, girls 108, and the hours of study are seven daily. There is no play ground. Rooms are warmed by open grates. The WC and privy are outside the building emptying into a cess-pool, the urinal passes into the street gutter.[9]

By the middle of the 19th century, the School had survived with mixed success under a number of more or less satisfactory Headmasters, until the coming of Thomas Slade, 'a sharp man with a keen eye'.

There is a vivid description of Slade's ideas on discipline and corporal punishment, but he no doubt had good reason for his attitude, for there would have been few, if any, assistant staff available to help him, the Beneficial School (in common with many others) working on the 'Madras' or 'monitor'system.

As its name implies, this system hailed from India and came into being in 1789, when a shortage of qualified teachers inspired a Church of England Minister, Andrew Bell, into developing the scheme of using older children to teach the younger ones; the method was later introduced into England and became widespread, until replaced by the 'private class' system.

However amateur and irregular the teaching under this system, it did at least ensure that Thomas Slade was offering a modicum of education to the maximum number of boys, and though, by today's standards, he might be considered harsh if not positively cruel to the pupils in his charge, he was an able and progressive Headmaster. And it was he who proposed the introduction of a girl's school, an idea taken up by the Society and put into effect early in 1837. A year later, and thanks to the 'Madras' system, Slade could rightly claim that 280 boys and 136 girls were being educated at the Beneficial School.

By the time he left in 1852, he had established the basis of a reputation that the School was to maintain right to the end of its career. He had abandoned the ' Madras' system in favour of 'private class' teaching (for which pupils were required to pay 3d. per week instead of the customary 1d.), and ten years later the School became involved in a vigorous updating project introduced by his son, James J. Slade. It survived competition from the Board Schools and even coped with the upheaval of the 1870 Education Act.[10]

Overcome by the demands made by HM Inspectors, James Slade was not to stay long, and a further four Headmasters followed, tackling the problems of the day, but by the turn of the century the School had become in all its facets little more than another typical Elementary School.

It must be said, though, that many of the scholars were to bring great credit to the School, the most notable of which must surely be Sir Henry Ayres, KC, MG, one-time Premier of Australia, after whom Ayres Rock is named. A fervent sense of duty, respect and loyalty to the Sovereign was instilled into every scholar, and is best indicated by Thomas Mariner's ambition for the pupils, that:

> by inculcating the patriotic and truly British feeling of loyalty to their King, and the love of their country . . . they may come, in their day, to be beneficial to their country and to the world.[11]

But in 1933 the Beneficial Society closed its doors and, accepting that in State education there was no longer a place for the Beneficial School, that too was closed down in 1938.

Thousands of boys and girls were to be grateful for the start in life they received at the Beneficial School, but it had taken the example of John Pounds and his pioneering Ragged School to bring about the first brave attempt to teach the really destitute children and it was thanks to him and his supporters that the 'Ragged School Union' had come into being in 1844, the first Free Ragged School opening in St. George's Square some twelve years later.

Portsmouth and Portsea Free Ragged Schools

A Report on the Portsmouth and Portsea Free Ragged Schools was submitted annually to its subscribers, beginning on many occasions with a brief outline of the history of the Schools.[12]

They were founded in 1849 by a few well-intentioned members of the community, lodged in premises occupied by a Mr.Totterdale in St. George's Square. This accommodation was soon to prove inadequate, however, and seven years later a new building was erected in Richmond Place, Portsea, immediately behind the St. George's Brewery. The Schools were supervised by a Master and a Matron 'Under the control of a Committee of 27 persons, assisted by 18 Ladies'. For many years the Ragged Schools had 'stood alone in their Charitable work'; there was no charge for teaching received, and only the truly destitute were admitted, and in an effort to improve the lot of the children, the Committee regularly issued a plea for food and clothing, citing as an example 'one gentleman especially having provided nearly all the boys who need them with shoes'.

In the Report of 1861, it was noted that the Master, Mr. Collins, 'fills the post with satisfaction', receiving £420.0. per annum, for his efforts, while Mrs. Stallard, the Matron is paid £176.0. a year – though two years later 'the majority of the Ladies Committee having determined that Mrs. Stallard should be dismissed it is resolved that notice shall be given to her that her services will not be required after Jany. 25th 1864'. No reason was given, but in the February the new Matron, Mrs. Wilson, was engaged as Matron and Teacher, while her adopted daughter, Annie, was to be employed as Assistant Teacher. Financially, Mrs. Wilson did better than her predecessor, being paid £20 per annum – but poor Annie was to receive a mere £5.

Average attendance at the time of the 1861 Report was 'Boys – 90, Girls – 55', with about fifty of the children being fed daily. There was a religious service held on Sunday mornings, but this was for boys only, there being no room for the girls!

As a result of their education, many of the 'ragged' children went on to occupy 'respectable and influential situations in the world – others are doing well in the Navy and Army. . . None during the time of their schooling have been brought before the Magistrates' – a fact for which the Committee was duly thankful.

Two years later, in 1863, the Report mentions that four boys were employed as Shoe Blacks at an average of 7s. per week; they received one third of their earnings, the rest to be 'expended in clothing for their use', until a year later 'it was determined That a rule Should be added to the rules for the Shoe Black Brigade to withhold 1/10 of their earnings for the purpose of buying blacking, brushes etc.'. This curious group, this 'Shoe Black Brigade' was in its way an elite, for whom there were a

RULES.

For the Guidance of the Parents of the Children

ATTENDING THE

PORTSEA FREE RAGGED SCHOOLS.

1.—The Children to be sent clean, and in good time, boys to have their hair cut short.

2.—No child to be sent if there is any infectious disorder in the family.

3.—Parents are to make complaints, if there should be any reason for them, only to the Secretary or managing Sub-Committee—not to the Master or Mistress.

4.—Parents must ask for leave of absence, or give good reason for the same, or the child will not be allowed to remain in the School.

5.—The Master or Mistress may refuse to allow a child to attend the School, if guilty of the breach of any of the above Rules, or of misconduct, but shall report the case immediately to the Secretary.

6.—The Parents shall have their children sent to a Sunday School regularly.

W. WOODWARD, 17, THE HARD.

Rules for the Guidance of Parents…
(PCRO)

few but nonetheless strict rules and for these boys fear of dismissal must have been constantly at the back of their minds.

Not only did the children receive an education but they (and some of their parents) were also fed at the School; for it is recorded that in 1865 Mrs. Wilson was authorised to 'carry on the Soup Kitchen for the supply of soup to the poor, to be made and given out at the School'. To make sure that subscribers to the School's funds need have no fear that their money was being misused, a separate fund was to be set up to pay for this, 'and no expenses to be thrown upon the School funds'.

By 1870 the Committee was able to claim that sufficient money had been raised for the provision of dinners on three days a week from January to Midsummer (a total of 850 a week), and for two days a week for the rest of the year. Of the Soup Kitchen, it was said 'Great demand for the soup tickets has proved how much many poor families have been assisted by it', and with these same people in mind, the Clothing Club had done much to help out, while the Treasurer, Mr. G.E. Gittens, had organised a Coal Charity, which had distributed twelve tons amongst the poor.

On one occasion in 1865 there seems to have been some trouble brewing, resulting in a request that 'Mrs. Wilson be relieved of all duty in connexion with the Sunday School'; however, the Rev. J.D. Platt, the Chairman and Incumbent of Holy Trinity, 'desired that Mrs. Wilson be referred to him' since the Sunday School was his concern. Matters did not rest there, for the Secretary was directed to ask Mrs. Wilson and Mr. Collins, the Master, to speak to him about the differences between them – and, quite incidentally, he was at the same time to take steps to stop the communication between the Boys' Schoolroom and the Girls' Staircase. . .

The Elementary Education Act of 1870 was unanimously adopted by the Council at a meeting held on 5 December. Members had learned that 8,000 children in the town were without any schooling whatsoever, and, anxious to correct this state of affairs, they set up the first School Board early in the following January.[13] However the introduction of the Act had caused considerable concern for many people, not least the Chairman of the Ragged Schools Board, Mr. Platt, who was worried by the thought of secular education being severed from religious teaching, and who also observed that '...if they introduced a system which could cast the whole burden of the expenses upon the Government they would have some cause to complain when the tax gatherer came round on the 1st of January'. This comment caused some laughter among his listeners, but he went on quite seriously to insist that he did not think compulsory attendance at school would 'exactly suit the English frame of mind'. But in spite of this, the School Board went ahead with plans for opening six new schools, the first in Chance Street in 1872.

In the years that followed the Ragged Schools Committee was to be haunted by visits from H.M. Inspectors, fearful of adverse reports. Initially, there was a delay of some *four years* in the receipt of the Inspectors' comments, causing the Committee to table a strong protest when the School was reported as being inefficient, but after a second examination, the Boys School was found to be acceptable. The Girls' School however failed the Inspector's test, though it was thought that this was mostly the result of a shortage of funds. There was some suggestion that the Boys' School be closed, but the Chairman had resisted this, paying out £30 to keep it open, and he appealed to those who 'believe in the benefit arising out of the union of religious and secular instruction' in schools. Church Schools, he was quoted as saying, are built 'for the purpose of Securing to the poor of the Borough an Education based on the principles of the Church of England. An Income of £100 is more than Sufficient to Ensure their Continuance and Efficiency', and the Committee appealed for help to 'Supporters of Religious Education for the poor'.

The threat of being 'Inefficient' was to hang over the heads of the Committee for some time to come, as witness the letter from the Secretary of the School Board, headed 'Portsmouth 20th March 1875', which set out to explain the problems of the Girls' School as he saw them. After a lengthy preamble, he wrote:

> I may however inform you that the Chief reason of the Girls Department having been rejected was the utter failure of the Scholars in Arithmetic. Unless therefore a competent Teacher be appointed I shall be obliged as and after the 1st of May next to treat the School as Inefficient and order the Attendance of the Scholars Elsewhere.
> I am, Yrs. faithfully, Robt. O. Spencer.

The Committee wasted no time in appointing the 'competent Teacher', a Miss Mary Alice Trode, who, on 3 May, 'commenced her duties as Teacher; took all the children under 7 years of age into the class-room'[14] – but her time at the School was limited, the Ladies Committee again finding fault and recommending her discharge.

She managed to survive for some five months, but by 13 September the Master observed that he 'found Alice Trode quite incompetent to teach arithmetic in the first class', and ten days later she was reported as arriving '40 minutes late in the morning'. Poor Alice Trode – whatever her shortcomings, she was the subject of a 'Meeting of the Gentlemen's Committee at 4 P.M.' when it was decided that 'Alice M. Trode be dismissed at Christmas as she is not qualified to teach the children'. There was a suggestion that it might be preferable to replace her with two assistants from the senior girls, at 1s. 6d. and 1s. per week respectively, but apparently this idea was not well received.

On Wednesday 22 December, there were 'no registers marked, as the children assembled at 2 P.M. only to partake of the usual Christmas treat of plum pudding and oranges. Clothing given to every child, the most deserving having two or three garments'. And while everyone else was no doubt looking forward to this rare excitement, there was one unfortunate who had little to be cheerful about, for there followed the comment that 'Alice Trode leaves today'. . . .

At a meeting of the Management Committee in March 1877, the Government Inspector's Report observed that '. . . the girls have a particularly clean and neat appearance . . . The weak part of the School is the Infants . . . ', and nine months later he commented:

> The removal of the Infants to a room of their own has been a very great gain to the Mistress. The girls are as last year particularly clean and well-behaved, and are in good order. The results of the examination, however, are not satisfactory. The failures are too numerous in all classes and in all subjects. Needlework is not clean. Geography was a complete failure. The Mistress requires the assistance of an older and better Monitor. . . The Infants are in capital order, and do great credit to their young Teacher. The younger Infants appear to learn but little; the older ones are fairly advanced, but should have better slates. They read well.

In a later report the Inspector comments on the Reading 'which is very monotonous in all Classes' and draws attention to 'the Writing of the first Standard; to the spelling of the second Standard, and to the Multiplication Tables in the first Standard'. And he 'cannot help thinking that the discipline is not as good as it used to be'. By 1889 there is little change:

> Arithmetic is fairly satisfactory, in the second, third and fifth Standard, but in the first and fourth it is almost a complete failure. Needlework, I regret to find is decidedly poor. . .

As to Infants' Mental Arithmetic, 'the children must not use their fingers' and 'Marching should be in step'.

As well as being hard pressed for adequate accommodation in such schools, there was only rudimentary sanitation and ventilation. The Ragged School received its supply of water as a gift from the Water Company, but others were less fortunate, mains water being seldom

available. Lighting, if it existed at all, was primitive and until 1855 the
Ragged School closed at 3.30p.m. in winter, the time lost being made up
in the dinner period.

As one example of the poor conditions in existence at the time, the
Medical Officer of Health's Report to the Committee in October 1878
drew attention to the unsatisfactory state of the drainage at the Ragged
Schools:

> Dear Sir,
> I should have written to you before about the School but I
> was trying to obtain some information about an old drain
> which as you will see from the enclosed plan runs or ran
> under the School. I have found out that it had been filled up
> in Mr. Lush's property but I do not know if this has been done
> under the School probably not as I recollect that the Schools
> were built long before the drainage was commenced if this
> old drain exists it should be filled up. The sinks should all be
> disconnected from the sewer and made to fall upon gulleys
> outside the buildings. The overflow of the cistern at present
> runs into the W.C. in the Master's house this must be altered.
> The cistern supplying the W.C. is also used for drinking pur-
> poses in the Master's house this is wrong. The pipe from the
> sink in the Master's house runs inside the buildings and some
> of the pipes are not tight this must be altered the sink must
> be disconnected from the drain and the pipe must be outside
> the buildings... The soil pipe of the Master's W.C. is inside
> buildings
> it should be outside.
> All drinking water should be drawn directly
> from the main.
> I am sir Your Obt. Servant
> Geo. Turner MOH.

This should have been sufficient to make any committee take steps to
improve matters, but in fact action was deferred on the grounds that
the Master's house was unoccupied at the time. There was a note to the
effect that one of Mrs. Ford's children[15] 'had typhoid but being re-
covered her Medic. Attdt., Dr. Way, said there was no further fear of
infection'; and another stated that the Schools had been closed but
were now to reopen – though there is no positive effort to relate these
points to each other.

By 1903 the Minutes had been reduced to a bare minimum, giving
little or no insight into the day-to-day activities of the Schools. But at
the meeting in June 1909, the managers were obliged to discuss the

question of better accommodation, and eventually they resolved that:

> Mr. J. Croad be asked to confer with the surveyor of the
> Education Authority . . . to advise as to the provision of
> accommodation to prevent the numbers of scholars being
> reduced owing to the alteration of the Education Depart-
> ment's requirements of 10 feet space for each scholar.

They had hoped to extend the building into the area of Milldam
Barracks, but this idea was rejected by the military authorities.

As further evidence of the Education Authority's involvement, the
managers had arranged for the Authority to take over the insurance of
teachers and paid staff, and they were also planning a scheme of
insurance to cover them against children being involved in an accident
on School premises, 'for which the Managers could be held liable to
compensation'.

Portsmouth and Portsea Free Ragged Schools
Log Book 1875-1893[16]

The school log book was kept for the benefit of the managers, inspectors and anyone else likely to question the efficiency of the Master, and
in consequence there are frequent observations such as 'Worked by
time table' or 'Progress ordinary'; often there was 'Needlework in the
afternoon' or a note that they had 'Practised School songs'. And at the
end of each week there was the obligatory report on attendance –
'Average for the week 74' followed by the percentage absence.

Weather conditions and the time of year undoubtedly had a big effect
on absenteeism, for while on 4 June 1875 'several children (were) away
from school this week with chickenpox', on the 21 June there was 'Very
small attendance (56) in the morning owing to heavy rain, rather better
in the afternoon'. On 14 July there was 'More heavy rain and small
attendance' followed next day with 'Attendance today very small as the
weather is even worse than yesterday', and continuing thus for yet a
third day. In October, there was 'Heavy rain and small attendance' for a
matter of some five days.

The Sunday school treat was another reason for the children being
away from school, but though this was invariably with the Master's
leave of absence, he could not have been too pleased on the day
following one such excursion, obliged as he was to write 'Attendance
very small (68) in consequence of the children being very tired from
their holiday yesterday'.

One entry, made in September 1877, illustrates (with perhaps uncon-
scious humour) the curious variety of events that governed the conduct
of the School:

> Small attendance, partly, owing to the children whose parents receive parish relief having to appear before the Board of Guardians, and partly to an attractive Circus procession through the town'. .

Visitors came to the School with rather tiresome frequency, most of them members of the Committee, and many showing a personal interest in the children to the extent of donating money for books, or linsey and calico for 'garments for winter' or, as in the case of a Miss Eastwood, sending '61 yards of linsey to be made into frocks for Winter'. This generosity was no doubt most welcome, but it could be a mixed blessing, as shown in the entry on 15 November:

> Usual attendance, worked at lessons in the morning, but must devote afternoon instruction to needlework, from now until Christmas in order to make up all the materials into garments'.

Some of these visitors would actually conduct a class themselves, and grateful though the teaching staff may have been for their support, it must have been somewhat unnerving, particularly for the young and sometimes 'uncertificated' monitors when one or more of the ladies elected to sit in on a class while they listened to the children read or take dictation.

At Christmas, the children learned carols, and from time to time they learned a new school song or a piece of poetry. In one year (1883) 'Songs taught for the Examination' show vividly the spirit of the age, a mixture of patriotism, duty and more than a touch of sentiment :

> The Polar Star
> The Emigrant's Farewell
> My Own Native Land
> Steer Onward
> O Sweet to Remember
> Never, Never say "Tomorrow"
> Christmas Bells
> The Robin.

New Year 1894 started with a new Log Book, with a neat list of the teaching staff, a not-so-neat list of the classroom measurements, a list of 'Recitations for 1894' and another, at first unexplained, a list of 'Gallery Lessons' – three columns of ten items such as:

> Elephant Coal   Potato
> Reindeer   Iron   Summer

Horse	Cotton	Winter
Whale	Apple	Clothing
Lion	Tree	Post Office

These turned out to be a 'List of Object Lessons for Infant Class', a title which only partly clarifies the matter. The recitations included 'The Vain Chicken' (for Standard I), 'The Inchcape Bell' (Standards II and III) and 'The Merchant of Venice' for the seniors in Standards IV and V.

'Mr. Crowley visited and warned children that they would not be allowed to attend school unless they were punctual'. This warning, issued in January 1894, was followed a week later by the note that 'Mr. Crowley . . . brought papers to be distributed among the most irregular children to obtain the parents cooperation in maintaining more regular and punctual attendance'. Mr. Crowley would seem to have been a tower of strength in his support of discipline, for in the June, 'One of the Mothers came in an abusive manner and took a girl out of the school who had been kept in for punishment. The Revd. C. Crowley . . . sent a message to the mother telling her the girl would not be allowed to return to school unless an apology was made'.

The years after 1900 saw many occasions when the school was closed for one reason or another . There was 'the Election' on 4 May, and the 'General Election' in September; again in May, the school was closed on two successive days – Ascension Day on 24th and 'in honour of Relief of Mafeking' on the 25th, while five months later they were given a half holiday 'in honour of (the) Volunteers' return from South Africa.

In July the percentage of absentees was 'higher this week than for a long time owing to the number of Sunday School Treats', and in September the Infant School was closed for a week, this time because 'part of the ceiling fell down on Monday morning'.

There were at this time several cases of typhoid fever, and one of the staff, Mrs. Graham was absent (after several visits to the doctor, duly noted in the Log book) said to be suffering with enteric fever.

One of the good things of 1900 occurred in October, when the School 'received notice of Cookery Classes for Girls to start on Wednesday November 13th from the Clerk of the Portsmouth School Board', and a week later it had been arranged that the 'Girls go to Cookery on Tuesday afternoon and Thursday morning' - an excellent idea, since a large proportion of girls would have gone into 'service' when they left school.

Little mention was made of wartime conditions. There was a Fire Drill in 1915, and in 1917 'War Savings Certificate Association started in this School on Monday January 8th'. A half holiday, 'by order of the Vicar, the Rev. C.H. Hamilton', celebrated the signing of the Armistice; another a week later allowed the children to see the Military War Procession –

by order of the Education Committee, and in early December there was a half holiday 'in honour of the Arrival of Surrendered German Submarines and other Craft'. Apart from this (and the Children's Victory Peace Demonstration in the following summer), the war would appear to have had little impact on the School.

Form-filling had become a fact of life, as indicated in an entry toward the end of the War: 'Received Form 9E (in triplicate) from Education Committee's Office this morning per Caretaker', and the Head Teacher seemed forever to be attending meetings: on 7 December, 'Manager's Meeting on Tuesday morning at 10.15 o'clock. A Ladies Committeee Meeting held on Tuesday morning at 11 o'clock'. As if this were not enough intereference with the School's routine, in the June of next year, the Committee's Inspector, a Mr. Richards, 'arranged for Miss C.M. Brook to be lent for duties at the Town Hall in connection with the issuing of the new Food Ration Books'.

There was one visitor, a Mr. Joliffe, who was scheduled to arrive at the School on 2nd December 1916 'for the purposes of giving a Lecture to Scholars in Standards 5.6. and 7 on the Physiological effects of Alcohol'. The objective was highly laudable, and it would seem the Authorities agreed, for he returned to the School year after year to give the same talk, a fact which must have become a little tiresome to those who were repeatedly required to sit through it. . .

In January 1921 the War Office gave permission to the Free School 'to use the parade ground of the Milldam Barracks at any time between an hour after sunrise and an hour before sunset. The wall is now being altered to hold a gate between the School playground and the parade ground'. By 1924 there was a school library, and books for the library were 'to be given henceforth by the Committee in place of prizes'. To give further breadth to the children's perspective, hobbies competitions were set up, and a swimming class was formed, while each year student teachers from the Teacher Training College came to the School to work out their period of teacher training.

In October 1924, the Head Teacher had 'received notice to send 36 children to South Parade Pier to witness a performance of *Merchant of Venice* on the afternoon of Friday november 21st under Art. 44 of the code'. This was to become an annual affair, for in 1925 they were taken to see *Midsummer Night's Dream*, and on another occasion, *As You Like It*. Clearly, it was now recognised that 'culture', and in particular Shakespeare, was respectable.

There is a privy in the room . . .

The original design of the eighteenth-century charity school provided for one large hall without any form of division, entered through a lobby which served also as the headmaster's room; where a school catered for both boys and girls, the building would be built on two storeys.

There was a single row of chairs laid out round three sides of the room, for scholars doing Writing or Arithmetic, while the rest were grouped in the centre, round one or more of the school 'monitors'. Discipline was severe, the children frequently having to stand up straight for most of the time, hands behind their backs or arms folded. Many years later the scene would appear to have changed very little, as Richard Esmond recalls in the description of his entry into school at the age of three:

> One room, taken up almost entirely by the "gallery". This was a sort of staircase ... (on which) the children sat in long rows. .. on an upward slope from floor almost to ceiling. .. Punishment was being shut in the dark under the gallery.[17]

A graphic description of conditions in school in 1850 appears in a report on the Day and Sunday Schools in Orange Street, submitted by Henry Slight:

> This is held in the body of an old Chapel, - and was founded in 1836-7. The Size is fifty feet by forty four and 14 feet in height. The average number of boys is 110, and the average hours of School five. There is no play ground. The Ventilation is effectd by the Windows and one Ventilator over the entrance door. . . The room is warmed by an open Grate or small Fire. There is a privy *in this room, which discharges into a Cess pool below the floor.* The Small Urinal runs into the Street gutter. . . The Ventilation is very bad and the rooms very dark – No Water is supplied to the Children. . . On my visit the atmosphere was very offensive with a damp musty smell (this was on Dec 11 - 1850).

His comments on the Girls' School are very similar; there is 'no play ground', the 'Water Closet is very offensive':

> The Children get Water from the Alms Houses above – which is the Portsmouth Water but the Alms women often refuse them. . . There is a small Yard behind through which passes a large drain, the Stagnant Water here is very offensive. So much so that the door is Seldom opened, the odour is so bad and the drain being too large Swarms with rats which often enter the School. This drain was cleaned during the panic from Cholera but has not been touched since.[18]

The Orange Street Chapel, post-Second World War.
(By courtesy of The News, Portsmouth)

It would appear that in respect of school accommodation if in nothing else the children in the Union Schools fared rather better than those in Orange Street:

> The Schools of the Union, in the ward of St. Mary, were founded in 1846. The boys room is 32 x 22ft., the girls 36 x 20, both 10ft high. There are large playgrounds. The daily hours of study are 8. the ventilation is good, and the rooms are warmed by fire grates. Pure water is obtained from a well 74 feet deep, and is carefully tanked and away from pollution. Privies and the urinals are distinct for each school and 100ft distant. Drainage is by barrel drains which empty into cesspools. . . the situation is healthy, and except for epidemics, the average sickness does not exceed 10 per annum. The education is most excellent. The ventilation by openings in walls, ceilings, and floors is perfect.[19]

In the opinion of a later Senior Education Officer, William Durman, this puts the Union School as outstandingly the best educational institution in Portsea Island at the time.

'A Scheme for Remodelling'

Accommodation in the schools after the First World War still left a great deal to be desired. For one thing, some had been requisitioned for use as military hospitals during the war years and were retained until 1920; for another, the population was being moved out of the poorer central areas to the outskirts of the town, leaving vacancies in the older schools while they caused considerable overcrowding in their new neighbourhood.[20]

Added to this imbalance, the actual structural condition of many schools was poor in the extreme. Apart from inadequate ventilation, lighting and sanitation, there was seldom sufficient playground area for the number of children in attendance, and the general design of the buildings was hopelessly out of date.

In 1924 William Durman tabled a notice to be brought before the Education Committee in February:

> That it be an instruction to the Sites and Buildings Sub-Committee to prepare a scheme for the remodelling of the older Elementary Schools of the Borough to embody as far as is possible the modern requirements of educational method in regard to:
> The size of class rooms.
> The separation of classes by adequate partitions.

Proper ventilation and heating.
Adequate storage for school apparatus, stationery and
books.
The provision of hygienic lavatory and sanitary conveniences.
The provision of proper facilities for physical and gymnastic
exercises,
and the substitution of electric for gas lighting.

The scheme was to be divided into two parts, initially to deal with
those schools in the worst condition, followed by the eventual updating
of all school buildings in the area. To emphasise the urgency, the notice
ended, 'The first part of the scheme shall be presented a month from
this date, the second within three months'.

It seemed at first that no one present in the Council Chamber was
going to respond to the motion, until the Vice-chairman rose to say he
was 'not going to let the mover. . . tell the public that the Committee
would not even discuss his motion', and agreed to second it.

Then, according to William Durman's own account, 'member after
member arose and described the beautiful palaces that existed for the
purpose of elementary education in Portsmouth, and . . . not a single
member spoke in (the motion's) favour' until the Chairman (Alderman
F.G.Foster) observed that 'it is unfortunately true that we have not done
all that could be done for the Elementary schools'. Urged to reconsider,
the Committee gave way, and the motion was eventually carried almost
unanimously.

The resultant survey was speeded up by the Board of Education's
demand that sanitary arrangements in several Portsmouth schools be
improved as soon as possible, the school in Kent Street being one of
these, and the Board also drew the Committee's attention to other
shortcomings mentioned in the letter sent to them as far back as 5 April
1913!

It is probably fair to say that the Committee was hag-ridden by the
need for economy throughout the 1920s, reducing progress to a minimum. Nevertheless several schemes for a general improvement of
standards were called for, including the building of two new elementary
schools, and new domestic science and handicraft centres. There was
some concern about the level of attainment among the older children,
many of whom it was thought were not being fully extended. One
relatively inexpensive innovation was introduced – the granting of
permission for teaching staff to conduct classes out of doors, where
feasible, and as a further step forward, some public playing fields and
recreation grounds were to be made available for physical education.

It was during this period that school journeys 'to places of historical
and otherwise educational value' were to be arranged, with special
grants made for children whose parents were unable to pay for these

outings. Immediately after the war there had even been a move to start up nursery schools, and Alderman Foster had offered accommodation in Edgcombe House in North Street for the purpose, but in spite of the enthusiasm for this idea, shortage of funds caused the scheme to fall through, to be shelved indefinitely.

Not until 1928 did a conference on 'Reorganisation' bring together all interested parties, to sort out the more urgent requirements for updating education in the City and, as a result of their work, in January 1929 the building of new schools was begun, with emphasis on the outlying districts such as Cosham, Farlington and Wymering, where so many Portsea families were now living.

Meanwhile the older schools, such as Kent Street, were to benefit from such modernisation as was practicable:

> The schools were wired for electric light; wherever it was possible central heating was installed; sanitary offices were brought into line with modern ideas of hygiene; ventilation was much improved; wherever possible play-grounds were enlarged, and thousands of pounds were expended in making the older ones fit for the youngsters to run about on; the abolition of double and treble classrooms was accomplished . . . and in all schools a head-teachers room was provided, together with a fairly generous provision of cupboards and stockrooms.

Further evidence of the changes taking place at the Kent Street School appears in the Report submitted by H.M. Inspector, Mr.F.A.B.Newman, on 29 and 31 May 1935:[21]

> Senior Boys
> 1. This school was reorganised in January 1934, but not until August last did it become a properly constituted Senior Department with an 11+ age of entry. As it draws its scholars from one of the poorest parts of the city, it is important that it should try to exert a civilising influence over them. It is doing this to an increasing extent under the quiet and steady guidance of the present Head Master who took charge about a year ago.
> 2. It may be said at once that, besides this improving atmosphere – evidenced by the tidier appearance of the boys and their books, and the greater effort they put forth – attainments, in the main, are also on the up-grade. A fair share of the credit for this must be accorded to the present Head Master's predecessors since 1930 when the school (then all-standard) had its last report. . .

Other improvements were to follow, including the Domestic Science building erected in 1938 on a site next to the Kent Street School, continuing right through to the start of the Second World War. In the words of William Durman, written in 1942:

> Slow as the advance (has) been since 1870 great changes have taken place; the illiterate person is a rarity today, in 1870 he was not the exception, but conformed to the general rule. By 1870 no working class child had entered a University, from Portsmouth, to-day it is rarely that a year passes without a score or more proceed from our secondary schools or college to London Oxford or Cambridge. In 1870 there was not a publicly provided secondary school for either boys or girls, and the only privately endowed secondary school was practically moribund.

But as the 'Clouds of War' grew darker and more threatening, it was the children who were going to feel the first and most immediate effect of the conflict.

PART IV

THE 'PREVENTION OF NUISANCE'

By the middle of the last century people were becoming aware that they had some responsibility for the health of those who lived in the more deplorable areas of Portsea. The Improvement Act of 1843 was a first sign of this awareness even if, as was so often the case, action and reaction were slow to take effect. Nevertheless, by its ruling the appointed Commissioners were give powers to improve living conditions, beginning with the widening of some streets, and by instigating improvements 'for the prevention of nuisances, for lighting, regulation of hackney coaches and porters', and allowed for:

> the levy (of) a paving rate of eightpence in the pound and another rate, called the Improvement Rate, not exceeding sixteen pence in the pound for the purposes of sweeping, cleansing, lighting, watering and improving the streets.[1]

For the people of Portsea there was no provision for health care beyond a dispensary in St. George's Square which could offer an assortment of medicines but little else, and it was a great and positive move forward when in 1845 a site in the Pitt Street area of Landport was granted on a peppercorn rent, the land to be used for the erection of the 'Portsmouth, Portsea and Gosport Hospital'.

The land was the property of the Board of Ordnance, the lease to last one thousand years, though it was stipulated that should the area be used for anything but a hospital the Board retained the right to repossess.

The first stage of the hospital was to provide twenty-five beds at a cost of £2,700, and the inauguration of the Royal Portsmouth Hospital in 1846 was followed the next year by the Prince Consort's visit to lay the foundation stone.

With the usual fulsome expressions of satisfaction, the Address written in honour of the occasion expressed the Council's 'pleasure in recognising in this act a desire to promote and . . . provide suitable means for the relief and succour of the suffering poor'[2]. This was not a moment too soon, for only a year later the first serious outbreak of cholera occurred, taking hold in Fountain Street and spreading rapidly through the poorer districts, eventually to reach epidemic proportions.

A newspaper cutting of 1849 deals with cholera under the heading: 'Plain Advice to All During the Visitation of the Cholera':

> It is the citizen's duty to avoid throwing refuse into the streets, nor to collect any in the back yard; there should be no dung heaps, no ash heaps; pigs should not be kept in close spaces; no sloppy holes in the backyard, and the yards should be levelled or paved. . . Tenants should insist that the landlord make houses watertight . . . If (there is) a foul ditch, or cesspool, stir yourself to have a change . . Have no poultry or rabbits within doors'.

There is a warning to be very careful not to drink impure water. 'Spend less money on beer and other drinks and spend more on flannel and coals', the people are told, for cholera can best be fought by keeping warm and avoiding getting wet.

The General Board of Health issued some further advice: 'Cholera . . . comes on with looseness or bowel complaint . . . Ardent spirits should be taken only under medical advice; drunkards always suffer most . . .'. Sufferers were advised to take a mixture of '20 grains of opiate confection, mixed with two tablespoonfuls of peppermint-water, or with a little weak brandy-and-water' and retire to a warm bed, with heated flannel applied to the stomach, feet and spine. 'Constant friction with flannel dipped in hot vinegar' is recommended, along with a vinegar and mustard poultice over the belly. This is followed by the promise that 'the humblest person will not send (for the doctor) in vain'.

Finally, 'Keep up your spirits, have no vain fears; relax no industry; shrink not from assisting your neighbours; and put your trust in Him in whose hands are the issues of life and death'.[3]

There is no indication of the writer of this article, but one cannot help observing that the very people to whom this might apply the most – the poor - would be both unable to read the instructions and unable to afford most of the recommendations contained therein. Special centres were set up in various parts of the town, to provide medical advice and treatment, and prayers had been said in every church and chapel, but even so, 800 victims of the cholera died and were buried in Kingston Churchyard, while at St. Thomas's Church in Portsmouth, the authorities were reduced to burying casualties in mass graves.

Over the years the Council was becoming increasingly aware of the growth of population throughout Portsea Island in general, and in 1852 formally adopted a petition stating that 'the Sanitary condition of the

Borough is such as to require the introduction of the Public Health Act without delay'. It was a bold proposition, meeting with resistance from the public, urged on by the Boards of Commissioners and within the month the Council conceded defeat and withdrew the petition; when it was tabled a second time, it was defeated by only two votes. Perhaps a study of the mortality figures strengthened their resolve, for in 1853 the the Council made yet another effort to adopt the Act and on this occasion succeeded, if only by a single vote.

The Public Health Act would have given the Council the power to control construction of drains and sewers, the disposal of refuse, and the regulation of 'offensive trades', slaughter houses, streets, dwellings, common lodging houses, etc.. They would be obliged to provide burial grounds and recreation grounds, to supply public baths, to protect the waterworks, and – among a number of other things – attend to the 'removing of nuisances'.[4]

The Act was meant to apply to the more populated areas, and, unless the mortality rate was exceptionally high, was only to operate at the request of local ratepayers. But, urged on by the Board of Commissioners (who feared they might lose their authority), the people of Portsea Island were reluctant to adopt the Act; their argument was against the expense of such an undertaking, since, at that time, the Government (or more precisely, the Navy and Army) paid nothing toward the rates, and not until 1860 was that liability accepted. It must surely have been a considerable disappointment to all those who had voted for the Act that even with a result in their favour, they were obliged to stand by and see the matter shelved indefinitely.

In 1872 smallpox[5] arrived on Portsea Island, spreading out to all corners regardless of individuals or their living condition and resulting eventually in the death of some five hundred and fourteen people. By October the Council, acting as Urban Sanitary Authority, considered the situation was bad enough to warrant a meeting with the Local Government Assistant Inspector, Mr. T.L.L. Murray Browne, to request him to submit a report and to offer such advice as may be helpful.

At the time there existed the establishment for four District Medical Officers of Health, though two of the posts were vacant and were temporarily in the charge of other local doctors, and in order to obtain a clear picture, Mr. Murray Browne requested each of the four gentlemen to submit returns to him. His letter to the Urban Sanitary Authority shows clearly the situation as it stood and his concern that it was going to get worse. There were, he says, twelve new cases reported that week, bringing the total to twenty-one:

> The above (figures) are of course exclusive of the patients
> under treatment in the small pox wards at the Workhouse

who on the 22nd inst. were in number 9. This makes in all 30 cases under Poor Law treatment. Dr. Diver further expresses a strong opinion that the disease is on the increase . . . (and) many persons carefully conceal the existence of the disease in their families. . . It appears . . . that small pox is not rife in Dr. Carter's district (Portsea).

Of the eight patients admitted to the Workhouse during the past three weeks six had come from Portsea. Since the disease was not rampant in this area Mr. Murray-Browne came to the conclusion that, much as people were repelled at the thought of being placed in the Workhouse, for whatever reasons, it had solved the problem in this instance:

> It is for the Urban Sanitary Authority to decide what steps shall be taken to meet it. I would venture however to press strongly upon their attention the following suggestions:
> 1. That a house or building in a suitable position should at once be hired to serve as a temporary small pox hospital for persons in a better station of life, leaving the workhouse wards (which accommodate only 24 and have already once in the course of the summer been more than full) to their proper office of receiving paupers only. . . It has the advantage of meeting the objection at present expressed (of) association with paupers, and the fear of being confounded with that class. . .

He urged the appointment of a temporary Medical Officer of Health, and his letter ended with the earnest plea that the Authority take immediate action to prevent the spread of the disease, and not allow themselves to be prejudiced in any way by the impending municial elections.

The Local Government Act of 1872 provided for many of the items listed under the Public Health Act, adding to them the need for a good water supply, inspection of food, registration of sickness and the regulation of markets, and in 1875 the Local Authority was required to appoint a Medical Officer of Health.

Further to the Inspector's comment about renting temporary accommodation, the Clerk to the Authority was ordered to contact Messrs. King and King and, not surprisingly, received the following reply:

> We regret we are unable to find any place at all likely either to suit you or to be let for such a purpose.

> We very much fear you will not find anyone willing to let premises for this and would almost suggest your obtaining a temporary building to be erected on some detached land . . .

While the Committee looked elsewhere for its temporary hospital accommodation, further problems arose when Dr. Davies reported in November that, in his district of Kingston and Landport:

> . . . I fear we shall have an Epidemic of Typhoid . . . no fewer than 13 cases of undoubted Typhoid . . . I fear that while the Drainage of the Borough continues to be in the very unsatisfactory State it is at present we shall hear more of Typhoid'

Dr. Rowe, standing in as Deputy for Dr. Carter, reported that in the past week in Portsea five cases of typhoid and sixteen of smallpox had been diagnosed. He added that there were no deaths, but he did not go into any detail - unlike his colleague, Dr. Diver, whose Report on 'the Railway District of Portsea Island Union' gives considerable insight into a dreadful situation:

> 1. 24 Mary Street Landport. A very mild case of small Pox, the patient a woman takes in mangling, she states that within the last few weeks, two persons. . . who take in washing for families at Southsea, having Small Pox in their houses, sent clothes belonging to their Customers to her (to) mangle , and that in one or both of these houses, the Case was so bad that death was the result.
>
>   I have ordered her not to take any more clothes for mangling during her sickness, She has nothing, she tells me, but her business to depend upon, and I respectfully suggest, that this is a case for some slight Compensation.

He stressed the matter of compensation on the grounds that, if this were available, 'it would encourage the poor to make known the fact that contagious diseases exist in their houses, instead (as they now do) of concealing the fact' while continuing their business.

There had been eleven smallpox cases admitted to the Portsea Island Union Hospital, ten of them from Portsea, and one from Landport:

> Viz.
> (1) Providence Court King Street (since dead)
> (2) Gospel Hall North Street
> (3) Queen Street
> (4) Seaman's and Marine's Orphans School
> (5) Lion Terrace

(6, 7, 8)
(9) Lion Terrace
(10) White's Row
(11) Landport, Paradise Street
. . . Two deaths have occurred in the Small Pox Hospital
during the past week, one of a boy aged 9 from Unicorn Street,
Portsea.

A young woman of nineteen had also died, her circumstances being
particularly sad, since she had volunteered to 'take charge of a Child, of
a woman who was sent into the Small Pox Hospital and there died'.

In Portsea a man of twenty-three from Frederick Street caught typhoid and died; in the same period, a young woman died of purpural
fever twelve hours after the birth of her baby, and a child of three
months died of syphilis, 'its blood being loaded with poison inherited
from its parents'.

Throughout November other Portsea cases were brought to the
notice of the Authority: a child living in Bishop Street, suffering from
typhoid, and severall smallpox cases, all of whom had died; a woman
aged forty from Providence Court, a woman of forty from Queen Street,
a woman aged twenty-three from Cumberland Street, and a boy of
fourteen from White's Row.

In the same month, November, the Inspector of Nuisances had
investigated the conditions in certain streets which had been brought
to his notice:

> Two were in a very filthy state, neither the roadway, pave-
> ment or gutter appear to have been properly made. (A third
> was) if possible worse than either of those named above, as
> in addition . . . the back yards of the houses are thoroughly
> impregnated with soil from the numerous cesspools (which)
> have to be emptied about every 3 months.

Other causes of both diseases, smallpox and typhoid, were 'water
standing in pools making the place almost impassable', and dust heaps
in front of the houses on which the inhabitants:

> throw all kinds of refuse including decaying vegetables (chief
> cause of Typhoid), privy full and in most often sour Condition
> during the bad weather the rain dilutes and washes a portion
> of the fluid contents into the Yard and escapes through an
> iron pipe which passes from the Yard through the rooms
> (above the boards) into the street emptying its contents in
> front of the doors. . . . this pipe leaks and at times a most
> offensive stench escapes and pervades their Common Living
> room'.

According to the minutes of the Urban Sanitary Authority, 'It is much to be regretted that power is not given by the Legislature . . . to order the isolation of all persons suffering from a disease like Smallpox'. But by December 1872 the 'diseases of the Zymotic Class' were on the decline, although there was still some fear expressed that unless a sharp frost set in, the heavy rain would prove a further hazard as vegetable matter rotted in the streets.

PART V

'CONFINED LIKE A FELON WITHOUT ANY CRIME. . .'

To have any understanding of the workhouse[2] and its place in the community one should perhaps have a look back to its origins, beginning with the meeting of the twenty 'discreet persons' who, in 1795, met at the *Pelican* inn at Speenhamland in Berkshire. At this meeting it was agreed that the current level of wages was frequently below subsistence level and it was proposed that wages should be made up to a basic minimum, the funds to come from the poor rate and to be set according to the price of bread and the size of the individual man's family.

The principle of this 'bread money' was widely adopted, regarded by many as some return for the enclosure of the poor man's common land, and therefore no more than his entitlement; at the same time Parliament was persuaded to repeal the ban on 'out-relief' and this, too, came to be regarded as a right. However, it was soon obvious that the Speenhamland system was open to every kind of abuse, among the labourers claiming this subsidy, among the farmers who no longer felt obliged to pay anything near a living wage, and among the Overseers of the Poor, many of whom (being local tradesmen) found the means to profit nicely from the movement of 'out-relief' money.

Over the years it became apparent that this misuse of funds was causing an intolerable increase in the poor rate; at the same time the farm labourer, agitated by the gradual introduction of machinery, rose up in protest, burning crops and destroying the new-fangled thresher that posed such a threat to his livelihood. The combination of these two factors brought home the need for rethinking the extent to which the better-off should help the undeserving poor who above all, it seemed, needed to be taught a lesson in self-support and family management before they reduced the whole country to poverty.

Experiment had shown that the best way to reduce the burden on the poor rates was to do away with 'out-relief' and to make 'indoor' relief deliberately unpleasant, to ensure that all but the truly 'necessitous' made every effort to get back into the outside world with the minimum of delay.

This did not please the pauper, for in his eyes it was still possible to retain one's self respect on 'out-relief' – and in any case, he objected to being housed with the 'lawless, drinking and worthless part of the community'. But within the workhouse itself, the rules were so strict, the accommodation so mean, that no man would willingly enter if he could possibly avoid it. To quote one of the first to introduce the construction of a Union workhouse, the Rev. John Becher of Southwell: 'The advantages resulting from a workhouse must arise not from keeping the poor in the house but from keeping them out of it', and George Lansbury's description of his first visit to a workhouse vividly sums up the current scene:

> . . . Officials, receiving ward, hard forms, whitewashed walls, keys dangling at the waist of those who spoke to you, huge books for name, history, etc., searching, and then stripped and bathed in a communal tub, and the final crowning indignity of being dressed in clothes which had been worn by lots of other people, hideous to look at, ill-fitting and coarse. . . Sick and aged, mentally deficient, lunatics, babies and children, able-bodied and tramps all herded together in one huge range of buildings. . . On one visit I inspected the supper of oatmeal porridge . . . served up with pieces of black stuff floating around. On examination we discovered it to be rat and mice manure.[3]

For years to come, the situation remained unchanged, the treatment of the poor harsh and frequently unjust, and abuse of out-relief threatening to impoverish the country, until eventually a Royal Commission was set up to investigate and to amend the existing laws. The result was the Poor Law Amendment Act of 1834, the essential points of which would be to ban all relief to the able-bodied and their families, except in the workhouse; to provide out-relief for the old and the 'impotent' poor (and this did not include the unsupported woman); and to undertake the merging of all parishes into a number of 'Unions', to be run by members of the various parishes and known as Guardians of the Poor, the whole to be supervised by a Central Board of Commissioners.

There were some people who feared that the workhouse might prove to be more attractive to the pauper than his own home, and means were devised to ensure that this would not be so: the inmate was to wear drab and unbecoming uniform, his work would be unreasonably hard and tedious, and worst of all, he would be separated from his wife and family under the new and rigid 'classification' rules. Popular opinion was divided between those in favour and those against the Act, but by 1839 all but 5% of the parishes throughout the country had accepted the idea of Unions.

Locally, the Act resulted in the amalgamation of the Portsmouth and Portsea workhouses into the Portsea Union, but this was only after considerable resistance from the people of Portsmouth. In 1836 they had registered their objection to such a Union with a downright refusal to nominate anyone to serve as Guardians, but eventually seven Guardians were elected for Portsmouth and fourteen for Portsea, the Rev. Edmund Dewdrey to act as their first Chairman.[4]

There followed some eight years of discussion regarding the need for a new workhouse, accommodation and administration clearly proving inadequate as things stood. In 1838 The Assistant Poor Law Commissioner, Mr. Hawley, had reported that 'the Governor was very reprehensible for the manner in which he kept them (the inmates) . . . and considered him together with the Matron, who appeared to take little interest in the management, as unfit to govern the establishment'. And on 13 May 1840 one of the Guardians, Mr. Pratt, drew the Board's attention to:

> The inconvenient situation of the Master's apartment at the Portsea Workhouse, which being situated in one corner of the building he had no command over any part of it.

In Mr. Pratt's opinion it should be in the centre where he could observe 'what was going on in every department', and the Board decided they would look into the matter at their next visit to the workhouse.

Later, in 1842, the Medical Officer, W.H. Garrington, was complaining bitterly about the size and ventilation of some of the rooms, and the fact that:

> . . .there is no spare room in the event of an extraordinary influx of Paupers or the breaking out of an epidemic in the House. The worst feature, however, in the Establishment is the Insane Department, which I should blush to show to anyone who had ever seen a well regulated asylum.[5]

The establishment of the Portsea Union brought little cheer to the paupers of Portsmouth who had previously enjoyed comparatively spacious accommodation, whereas now, with the coming of the Union they found themselves in what amounted to prison conditions. By contrast, the sick of Portsea were to benefit from the extra accommodation, now that the Portsmouth workhouse was to be run as a home for the ill and infirm. But lack of Parish funds restricted good intentions generally and the inmates of Portsmouth in particular were to feel the pinch.

As in most Unions, there was still an urgent need for a new work-house, due largely to the Commissioners determination to maintain the policy of 'classification', dividing the inmates into seven separate categories:

> 1. Men infirm through age or any other cause
> 2. Able-bodied males over fifteen
> 3. Boys between seven and fifteen
> 4. Women infirm through age or any other cause
> 5. Able-bodied females over fifteen
> 6. Girls between seven and fifteen
> 7. Children under seven.

To this the Commissioner added the rider:

> This separation must be entire and absolute between the sexes, who are to live, sleep and take their meals in totally distinct and separate parts of the building, with an enclosed yard for each.

The only exception to this deliberately harsh rule was in the case of 'infants (who) may be kept by the mothers until of age . . . to be sent to school'.[6]

The building of the new workhouse at Milton was at last undertaken, to be completed in 1846; initially there was considerably more room for everyone, but as with the majority of workhouses throughout the country, there was to be no let-up in the rules and regulations of such a large institution, particularly when – as happened in the year 1896 – there were as many as seventeen hundred 'necessitous' people packed into a building designed to hold a thousand.

Making ends meet was hard enough for some, even when the man of the house was working; for those unemployed the workhouse stood metaphorically 'just around the corner', a forceful reminder that if things were already pretty bad, they could get a whole lot worse.

Employment in Portsea was always unpredictable, work in the Dock-yard dependent upon the vagaries of international affairs and Admiralty requirements. Shopkeepers saw the level of that employment reflected in their sales – when the Dockyard was doing well, everyone did well; when numbers were run down, everyone felt the pinch. Who were these people driven to that last resort – admission to the workhouse?

They were the young men with a trade who had had the misfortune simply to fall on hard times, or the sick – particularly those with typhoid, scarlet fever or the dreaded smallpox, for whom there was nowhere else to go. There was the single girl who had 'got herself into trouble', thrown out by her family or her employer, driven babe in arms to seek assistance, and there was the old man, his wife and family gone, drifting from lodging house to lodging house until lack of funds obliged him to turn to the workhouse. And there was the tramp, the pedlar, the 'vagrant', picked up off the street and sent to the workhouse, only to be released on promise of 'going elsewhere'. All these people found themselves a place in the Porter's Admission and Discharge Book[7], or in the Creed Register.[8]

Such admissions were not confined to the bad days of the last century, for the names of old people, mostly men, still appear as recently as the 1930s. 'James' was admitted in 1937, single, a seaman nearly eighty years old; he claimed he had no relatives and he gave his address as No.2, St. George's Square, a lodging house kept by William Whymark. No reason was given for his having to leave his lodgings, but at least he was not alone in this – a week later, on 16 September, a widower of seventy from the same address who had been admitted to the workhouse, had discharged himself only to be re-admitted the next day. He, too, had no relatives – so had he returned to his 'permanent address', only to be turned out for want of a few shillings rent? Within the four weeks up to 12 October, there were two others from No.2 St. George's Square – 'Georgie', who was single, a labourer of seventy, and 'Alfred', seventy-four. The latter had a niece in Landport, but for whatever reason there was no place room for him at her home, leaving him the workhouse as the only alternative.

This lodging house was one of many, including one in Oyster Street kept by Henry Whymark, and this also housed many of the old men who were in the end obliged to find their way to the workhouse door.

Even sadder than these poor old men were the children relegated to workhouse life. One, born in November 1935, was sent to the workhouse while his mother was confined at the maternity ward of St. Mary's; his home was given as 181A, Queen Street, the property of James Thomson, and the boy's father was still living at that address; but presumably there was no one available to care for the boy while the mother was away. There is a note that toward the end of September he was 'readmitted from hospital', while his mother, Maisie, remained at St. Mary's – but that's all.

In 1937 Phillip and Douglas N - , three years old, were discharged on 23 September to go to the 'C.C. Homes, Cosham, c/o Mrs. Ellis'. And eight-month-old twins were brought in, their mother's address not known, since they had been living with a foster mother, the illegitimate sons of a hall-porter in Bournemouth. They were immediately removed to hospital, but what became of them later? Were they, too, despatched to the Children's Cottage Home in Cosham?

Over the years there was a stream of unfortunates for whom there was no alternative to the workhouse; most managed to discharge

All that remained of 2-4 St. George's Square, post-Second World War.
(City Secretariat, Portsmouth)

themselves in a matter of days, and some quite simply 'did not return from leave'. The steady influx from the Whymark lodgings and others similar continued right up to the outbreak of war, when, on 2 September 1939, eight of the inmates left suddenly at their own request, two 'did not return', while eight children, all under three years, were rapidly despatched to the safety of the Children's Cottage Home in Chichester.

The 3rd of September was a Sunday, with no activity in or out, but on 4 September another twelve people removed themselves with more to follow later that week, and those admitted were noticeably reduced in number; only one apparently came from Portsea, from St. George's House – but he too left a week later. Perhaps the Guardians were only too pleased to reduce numbers at this time, but from all the activity it seems clear that with the coming of war, no one liked the idea of staying on in the workhouse if they could possibly arrange to leave. . .

Overseers' Minutes 1900

The Overseers' Minutes Book provides many clues to the day-to-day running of the workhouse, not so much in the more routine entries – Orders of Removal, the Clerk's Examinations of the Master's Day Books, Receipt and Payment Books, etc. – but in the smaller 'Any Other Business' items. For example, on one occasion it was proposed:

> . . . that a special vote of thanks be accorded to Mr. J.W. Boughton for so kindly inviting the Children, Aged Inmates, and Imbeciles of the Workhouse and Infirmary to the Pantomime at the Theatre Royal.

It is heartening to learn that someone thought the innocent and the old were entitled to a real treat at a real theatre. But one wonders what could have been going on on another occasion to cause the House and Schools Committee to observe that having 'carefully considered the Chaplain's Report with regard to the entertainment given in the Chapel', they would have the right to veto 'anything which in their opinion might be of an improper nature'; but they were, however, content to leave the matter to the good sense of the Choir Managers, with the proviso that in future they 'must have heard each song before it is sung in the Chapel'.

Observing such niceties may well have been out of consideration for the ladies present. Since 1834 women had been eligible for a place on the Boards of Guardians, and though none was actually elected until 1875, by the turn of the century there was a total of two thousand of them throughout the country. Although they undoubtedly brought a more sympathetic attitude to the running of the workhouse, at the same time these women were true Victorians – and perhaps it was the women on the Portsea Union Board who so disapproved of the questionable songs sung in the Portsea Chapel?

At a meeting in March 1900, the Board tabled a proposal concerning the widows of lower ranks killed on active service, often driven to the workhouse for want of any obvious means of support:

> We the Guardians of this Union, are of the opinion that the time has arrived when the principle of pensioning the Widows and Orphans of Officers and Warrant Officers of the Sea and Land Forces of this country, should be extended to the Widows and Orphans of the Non-commissioned Officers and Privates of Her Majesty's Army, Petty Officers, Seamen and Marines of Her Majesty's Navy who have died, whilst in the service of the Crown . . .

It was intended to obtain the support of local Members of Parliament and all Boards of Guardians, but presumably not everyone was in favour; an amendment was carried recommending the proposal be forwarded to the Visiting Committee for approval before being sent on to higher authority, thus conveniently shelving the matter for the time being at least.

At this same meeting, the Chairman's Annual Statement brought more cheerful news, announcing that six boys from the workhouse had gone to join the Army, eight to the Navy, and six boys and seventeen girls into 'places of service'. The Training ship *Mercury* was accommodating seven boys at a cost of £21 per annum, which the Chairman considered was not only worth the expense involved but was 'most beneficial, as the chances of the lads ever returning to the Institution are very remote indeed'.

Perhaps the following was the most significant section of his Statement:

> On Saturday next the Portsea Island Union ceases to exist. On 18th July 1836 the Parishes of Portsea and Portsmouth were united for Poor Law purposes, and on the 20th March 1862, the Parish of Great Salterns was added . . . forming the Portsea Island Union.
>
> By the Portsmouth Corporation Act 1839 they are to be described as the Parish of Portsmouth, and the Guardians to be described as 'Guardians of the Poor of the Parish of Portsmouth'.

This pronouncement was dated 28 March 1900, and might reasonably be considered one small but vital step nearer the welfare State.

Rules re Diet

What sort of food were these paupers given to eat? With the picture of Oliver Twist in mind, it is easy to imagine they were fed exclusively on bread and some form of unappetising gruel, but the *Rules re Diet*[10] would suggest otherwise.

Whether the food were well cooked or not, whether it was well presented or doled out from large communal coppers, by the turn of the century the quantity and variety was most rigidly laid down and the Master was required to submit detailed returns, not only of food put before the inmates, but of any food left over that could be recycled and served again the following day. Not only this, but each man was entitled to demand that his portion of food be weighed on the table in front of him. Quantity and quality may have left much to be desired, but at least these rules did away with the idea of the wicked workhouse Master robbing the inmates of their ration.

It was typical of the stringent rules that:

> . . . no inmate shall have or consume any liquor or food or provision other than is allowed in the Dietary Table . . except on Christmas day, and, with our consent, on public holidays . . .

Furthermore, there was to be no 'fermented or spiritous liquor unless in pursuance of a written recommendation of the Medical Officer for the workhouse . . . these to be entered in the 'Alcohol Book''.

It was possible for inmates who were sick to be put on a special diet, as prescribed by the Medical Officer of the workhouse, or, if he were absent, by the Nurse in charge at the time; but there was a great deal of bureaucracy to be gone through, first by applying to the Master for the requisite diet, 'such requisition to be termed "Statim Requisition" shall be made, with counterfoil, in the Form marked C, in Schedule B to this Order'. Subsequently, the Nurse was required to produce the counterfoil for the Medical Officer to initial, and it would hardly be surprising if on occasion she decided the patient was not really so ill as to warrant such a performance.

Such bureaucracy had at least the virtue of accepting there were various categories of inmate to be considered; for instance: 'Persons of unsound mind; Women advanced in pregnancy; Women suckling infants, and Infants under the age of 3 years' could be allowed special treatment, provided it was approved by the Guardians.

For the purpose of allocating food, the paupers were divided into six categories:

Class 1: Men not employed in Work (Plain Diet)
Class 1A: Men employed in Work (Same Diet as for Class 1,

with an additional meal on week days only, to be given at
lunch or at such times as the Guardians may decide)
Class 2: Men not employed in Work (Infirm Diet)
Class 2A: Men employed in Work (Same Diet as Class 2, with
an additional meal on week days only, to be given at lunch or
at such times as the Guardians may decide)

Class 2B covered 'Feeble men' entitled to a special Infirm Diet, and
the remaining classes were the same as those above, applied to women.
Class 5 referred to children over three years of age and under eight, and
Class 6 to children over eight years and under sixteen.

There was one small concession given to children – that they should
be fed according to their appetite, 'and it shall therefore not be requisite to weigh each ration to each individual child'. However, 'no portion
of such total allowance shall be removed from the Dining Room until
after the conclusion of the meal . . ., when any portion remaining
unserved shall, if fit for future use, be weighed or measured and returned into store forthwith and duly accounted for'.

All food was itemised and numbered, and selections from the list
'shall be such that with the exception of boiled or roast beef meals no
two dinners shall be alike in the same week for any one Class. Roast
meat may be served cold 'if the Guardians so direct', and may be
minced for certain Classes 'who may not be able to masticate their food
without difficulty' – and there was a Form to cover these and any other
permutations on offer.

All in all, it would seem difficult to look upon the workhouse diet with
anything but a sneaking envy: there was for instance, mutton and
savoury mince and roast pork, there was boiled beef and boiled bacon,
and various soups – Pea, Lentil, Haricot and Barley. To follow there
could be Suet Pudding, Roley-Poley Pudding, Golden Pudding or Fresh
Fruit Pudding. Admittedly the quantities were somewhat meagre by
present standards, but 'Beef, boiled, 4-oz; Bread, 4oz; Potatoes or other
Vegetables 12oz' is nowhere near hardship level. Why then does the
uncomfortable feeling persist that all was not as it may seem . . .?

> *. . . Surrounded by walls that are too high to climb,*
> *Confined like a felon without any crime.*
> (Written from Newmarket Union, 1846)

PART VI

'OF CRIMINALS AND CRIME'

There were many factors contributing to the high level of crime in Portsea. With the end of the Napoleonic wars discharged soldiers and seamen roamed the crowded courts and alleys, nowhere else to go, while others, released from the Dockyard and unable to find work, took refuge in the mean lodging houses that abounded in the area. Prostitution and drunkenness were facts of life, and though many cases of smuggling were taken to Court, there were many more that never came light.[1]

Portsmouth's new Borough Gaol had been opened in 1808, tucked away in Penny Street, with the Sessions House immediately above the Gaol, a grim enough warning to the wrongdoer. There was a constant problem of overcrowding, as many as thirty to forty prisoners awaiting trial confined to a single dayroom, while some prisoners had to be farmed out to other gaols to relive pressure, but conditions did not noticably improve until years later, with the building of Kingston Prison in 1874.

The police force, poorly paid and totally inadequate for the level of crime prevailing, found their task almost impossible, and members of the force could expect little help from the people they were trying to serve; and together with prostitution, drunkenness and petty crime, juvenile delinquency was prevalent, the children probably urged on by penniless parents who would go to any lengths for the price of a meal.

Many of the convicts, in particular those awaiting transportation, had in the past been condemned to spend the period of their sentence in the Hulks moored in the harbour. In 1851, however, it was proposed that they be removed to a new convict prison, to be built near the Anchor Gate. This met with strong opposition from the people of Portsea, on the grounds that to establish such an institution in a densely populated area and close by the Dockyard would be an act of most injudicious folly. Public feeling ran so high that the Town Council eventually sent a petition to the Queen, but whatever her feelings on the subject, the prison was nevertheless built a year later.

There was room in the new gaol for over a thousand convicts, a chapel large enough to accommodate them all, and a school where they were given the basic rudiments of an education. Once they were safely installed in their new quarters, they were enlisted as labourers on new projects about the town – a fact which upset many of the unemployed who saw their own prospects of work diminishing; but at least the physical presence of the convicts in their new quarters failed after all to give any cause for concern, and they remained in this accommodation until 1895 when they were no longer required as a labour force.[2]

Accepting that the police were underpaid and the force undermanned, it is not too surprising if from time to time individual members were themselves to be accused of crime of one sort or another, whether this be from inadequate investigation, a simple case of momentary loss of temper or, more rarely, a genuine misdemeanour.

Examples of such unfortunate events emerge from the records of the Watch Committee[3]; for instance, on 3 January 1840 the Mayor and Magistrates 'found it necessary to dismiss William Braxton, one of the Sub-Inspectors, on a charge which had been clearly proved against him – 'receiving money for settling a dispute between two parties'.

There were rather frequent charges of drunkenness on duty, so many in fact that in June 1840 the Watch Committee issued a formal warning:

> With a view to preventing the crime of drunkenness in those employed in the Police force of the Borough . . . any man belonging to the force being brought before the Committee on a charge of drunkenness, which shall be satisfactorily proved, he will be peremptorily dismissed.

Not all Watch Committee business was involved with the misdeeds of its Police Force. They were for instance invited to take notice of a letter from the Clerk of the Board for Repairs of Highways in the Parish of Portsea, 'complaining of the injury done to the Highways by persons who collect manure, digging down the bank and widening the ditches'.

At a later meeting the Committee passed a vote of approbation to the members of the Force who were present at a fire on the premises of a Mr. Hatherly in St. Thomas Street, Landport, 'for the promptness and activity on the occasion'. The members of the Committee were somewhat alarmed when it was subsequently brought to their notice that the Alliance Insurance Company had paid the sum of 28s. to be distributed among the Police for their services at the fire. There is a suggestion of righteous indignation as the Town Clerk is directed to write to the Alliance agent, Mr. Low, and state that 'the Committee had not authorised any application for remuneration . . . but at the same time the Committee consider the Sum tendered by the Company to be very inadequate for the valuable services rendered by the police'.

The Superintendent was directed to return the money.

It is hardly surprising to learn that the occasional constable continues to get himself into trouble. However, according to the evidence available, one police officer in 1851 seems to have been extraordinarily unlucky, the poor man having attempted to do no more than what he saw to be his duty – and finishing up having to make application for assistance to the Board of Guardians.

The constable concerned was a William Moore, about whom William Devereux, the Clerk to the Board of Guardians' reported as follows:

Portsea Island Union, 13 January 1851[4]

Day of Weekly Meeting Wednesday William Devereux, Clerk
No.41, St. Mary's Street,
Portsmouth

Gentlemen,

A short time since one of the police named William Moore, applied to the Guardians for relief on account of his pay having been stopped for a fortnight, and on their enquiring into the cause of his application, he made a statement, a copy of which I enclose herewith.

There is no doubt that the man Butler did escape from those in whose care he had been placed, and the Guardians were willing to give him (crossed out) a compensation to the police-man if they could have done it with the prospect of its being allowed in their accounts, but as it could not be considered as relief to the Poor, the policeman being then in employ, they were under the necessity of dismissing the application.

The Board of Guardians have therefore directed me to submit his statement for your consideration.

I have the honour to be
Gentlemen
Your obedient Servant
W. Devereux
Clerk.

To the Watch Committee
of the Borough of Portsmouth

Attached to Devereux's report was William Moore's version of events:

Statement of William Moore

I was on duty on the 31st October last at the Station house, Portsea, at six o'clock in the Evening. I heard an outcry in Ordnance Row, and I went to the door of the Station house – I saw a man named Butler running towards the Station house – there was a crowd behind him, Butler came up, and immediately afterwards two men, who said to me, take care of this man, he is out of his mind, and we are sent from the Union to take care of him – he has knocked us both down and made his escape, and he has been running about with an open knife. If you will detain him, we will go to the relieving officer and see if we can get him into the Union house, as we are of no use. I put him into the cell to await their return. Shortly afterwards, his wife came to the Station and said, Police-man, get that knife from him, and in endeavouring to search him, he bit my thumb severely.

I reported to the Inspector what I had done, and Butler was detained all night. The relieving officer came to the Station house with a Surgeon the next morning, who said the man was insane, and he was taken to the Union House.

I Kept on duty for a fortnight, but on account of the bite I was compelled from the severity of it to be off duty for a fortnight afterwards, and my pay for that period has been stopped by the Superintendent who considered that I ought not to have interfered.

The man was making towards the door of the Station house, and I took him by the collar and asked him what he wanted. It was either at the door, or not more than a yard from it.

Prostitution was frequently brought to the notice of the Watch Committee, as in the August of that same year, when the members were resolved that 'the attention of the proper authorities be called to the disgraceful scene which occurs every Sunday on the passage of the Military along the Ramparts to and from Divine Service by the assemblage of prostitutes and other disorderly characters and referring particularly to the assemblage at Bistons Bastion'.

One such 'disorderly character', Nicholas Gorman[5], a painter, was found guilty of 'unlawfully attempting on 16th of January 1856, to persuade Thomas Chapman, a soldier in the Royal Regiment of Artillery, to desert therefrom' and for this, and for attempting to persuade a second man to do the same thing the next day, he received one year in gaol. This was apparently considered less reprehensible than the action of George Joseph Nathaniel Charlier, an ordnance clerk, who found himself arrested for 'Embezzling the sum of eleven hundred and sixty pounds, the monies of Her Majesty', and received five years' penal servitude for his crime.

Stealing continued to meet with harsh official disapproval, for although the days of hanging for sheep-stealing were a thing of the past, still the penalty for the more trivial offences could not be ignored. In August 1859, Margaret Thomas[6] appeared before the Magistrates, accused of taking 'from the person of the said Thomas Plummer Boyle a purse, Money, to wit, Six Shillings his Property contrary to the Statute in such cases made and provided and against the Peace of our Lady the Queen her Crown and dignity'. At the hearing Thomas Plummer Boyle, 'Superannuated Gunner from the Royal Navy', claimed he was accosted in Flathouse Road by 'the Prisoner' and 'another Female':

> . . . the Prisoner said "I know you are good natured you will stand me something to drink I said "You have the advantage of me, I don't know you, I must request you to walk about your business and allow me to pass"; during this time I felt the Prisoners hand near me right side Trowsers pocket. . . and with her other hand grasped hold of my Watch guard and attempted to take it . . . I put my hand to my right hand Trowser pocket and missed my purse in which there had been a ½ Crown a florin a Shilling and a Sixpence. . . As soon as I missed my purse I . . . said to her "You have robbed me of my purse"; she said "I have not I dont know you"; the other three Females who were with her closed round me when I charged the Prisoner with robbing me and pursued her (to) the corner of Cumberland Street Portsea and I then sent for the Police and gave her into custody. . . .

Faced with the evidence Margaret Thomas pleaded guilty and was 'thereupon convicted before us (the Magistrates) of the said offence' and found herself sentenced to 'be imprisoned in a House of Correction, of the said Borough, and there be kept to hard labour for the space of two calendar months'.

There are endless accounts of such petty thieving, so much of it a clear indication of the deplorable poverty of the time. There was the case of John Leach who on 23 October 1859 stole 'from the person of George Killuck a neckerchief and money, to wit three shillings and sixpence his Property', and received 'hard labour for the space of Twenty one days'. Ellen McNelly was arrested for the theft of a copper tea kettle, value 2s. 6d., for which she was given twenty-one days hard labour – even though she had admitted her guilt.

The case against Keziah Dunning and Elizabeth Miller would seem to have had an even harsher outcome, for they had stolen a pair of woman's goloshes, *value 1s. 6d.,* the property of Joseph Dodman,

The Apollo, Prison Ship, at Portsmouth Harbour, Aug.ᵗ 1825.

Cornwainer of 163 Queen Street. They, too, had admitted they were guilty, but it didn't save them for 'Conviction upon a Plea of Guilty' still meant they would be sent to a House of Correction for 21 days' hard labour.

'Drunk and Disorderly' was the most common charge, those concerned being as often as not women, frequently prostitutes, who would be detained for a matter of some seven to ten hours to cool off and then discharged. These same women would not be above thieving, given the opportunity; but the owner of the stolen property frequently decided against following up the complaint, particularly if they had allowed themselves to be relieved of quite trivial articles in questionable circumstances. A certain Ellen Vickery, for instance, was charged with 'Pawning 3 Shirt Studs the property of Lieut. Johnson R.N.'; perhaps it is not surprising that the prosecutor failed to appear, and in consequence the young lady was discharged.

The police were active in seeing that licensing hours were, if not rigidly observed, at least given some degree of respect , and there were many instances of the police entering a public house and reporting law-breakers, much as they did in January 1848, in a full-page write-up concerning a certain Mary Ann Newman, :

> Sunday Morning ½ Past 11 o'Clock Visited the Publick House Known as the Sign of the Hat in Hand Situated in Camden Ally (*sic*) Kept by Mary Ann Newman found Seven Men in the Tap Room 2 quart Mugs on the Table with beer 4 Pint Mugs with Beer in them 3 Men Smoking.

One landlord, David Callender, was either consistently careless or consistently unlucky, for he was reported for breaking the licensing laws on three occasions. In December 1848, at twelve midnight, two police constables visited 'the Beer Shop Kept by Mr. David Callender situated in Bishop Street found 4 Men, 1 Woman in the Tap Room 2 Men Smoking 1 Quart Mug with Beer & 2 Glasses with Beer'. He was caught again six month later on 16 June and for a third time on 8 July. But he was by no means alone – George Giles, who kept the 'Beer House Known by the Sign of the Victory' in Butcher Street, was fined 2s. 6d. with 11s. costs, and in the following June, in the course of a single week, other 'Beer Houses', in North Street, Albion Street and St. Mary Street (Portsmouth) received similar visitations, the landlords having to pay similar fines.

In this same Report Book there are the sad things, like the poor man, 'Joseph Jacobs charged as a wandering Lunatic' and sent to the Asylum: there are comic entries, such as 'James Vogalsang charged with Stealing Six Geese and one Turkey', the property of a Madame Duboise: and there are trivial events , as for instance the finding of the 'side door of house in Queen Street open. Called the owner who got up and made it fast, Said the Servant must have Left the door open'. On occasion the police had to be called in to assist at the location of a fire, as happened one October:

> . . .between the hours of 7 and 8 o'clock in Stables occupied by Mr. John Gurd situated in Aylward Street Portsea. Inspector Martell and 2 police constables attended with Portsea Engine and Engine from Dockyard.

There was apparently very little damage caused to the premises 'but the loss of a valuable Horse, the property of Mrs. Gurd', and it was thought that the fire had originated with a lighted candle falling among the straw.

As late as 1856 prisoners were still occasionally whipped. Henry Booth, an illiterate, caught 'stealing from Land' was sentenced to receive three months imprisonment and be whipped, while Joshua Sturges, aged 13, for 'stealing from Land' was given twenty-one days' imprisonment and whipped. Two other boys aged 14, one of 15 and one of 17, were all sentenced to three months and whipped; all but one of these were illiterate. Perhaps one of the harshest sentences handed down at this time occurred in February 1857, when three boys, aged 11, 12 and 13 were arrested for vagrancy and were sentenced to fourteen days' imprisonment and three years in the Hampshire Reformatory.[7]

One of the more likely causes of trouble would be the result of soldiers and seamen coming to blows, particularly after a night out; an incident which might ordinarily result in a brief appearance in Court and a cautionary word from the Authorities would usually put an end to the matter, but the 'Fatal Affray' in White's Row was to prove far more serious than a mere street brawl.

The incident occurred late one night in January 1860, when a group of seamen and Dockyard workers, gathered together in a beerhouse in White's Row, came face to face with with a number of men from the Limerick Militia. There was a row – possibly to do with the women who had been sitting with the sailors; and the mood was not improved when someone decided to douse the lights.

Far from cooling the situation, tempers became more inflamed; fighting was carried on into the streets and in the ensuing confusion one man – a boilermaker called Daniel Clewney - was mortally wounded. *The Hampshire Telegraph* commented on both the scenario and the outcome:

> White's Row, the scene of abominations which neither the mind can conceive nor the pen describe, may now have

'Original photograph taken in Portsmouth Gaol, 1900...'
(PCL. Photograph D.G. Dine)

added to its dismal category the crime of murder. A party of men assemble in one of the pest houses of that miserable thoroughfare where morality is unknown, a quarrel ensues upon ludicrously trivial grounds, a brief but determined fight ensues, and ere minutes have elapsed, one of the party is a corpse.[8]

For all that, two of the accused were acquitted, three sentenced to four years' penal servitude - light sentences, one would think, compared with some . . .

Death of 'My Georgie'

In July 1922 Annie Smith lived at 39A Unicorn Street, Portsea. She was a single parent, employed at the corset factory in Buckland, a decent, hardworking woman, separated from her sea-going husband. Her small son, Georgie, spent much of his time at his Grandmother's house, and that was where Annie last saw him, sitting on the kerb outside, a cheerful little three-year-old dressed in striped blouse, navy blue serge knickers and black shoes and socks.

When she came back from work at tea-time the boy was missing; concerned, she went to look for him, asking up and down the street if anyone had seen 'My Georgie'[9]. And when no one could throw any light on the mystery she turned in panic to the police, begging for their assistance.

The first clue came from John Ryan, an old soldier living in the same street, who told how the boy had begged him for a halfpenny to buy sweets; the two of them had gone to a shop in Orange Street where he'd bought a shilling's worth of sweets and given a handful to the boy. The owner of the sweet shop, a Mr. Baker, confirmed the story, adding that when Georgie left the shop he had run off to play with a group of boys nearby.

Nothing more was heard, though rumours persisted – that he had gone to The Hard, fallen in the water and drowned, or that he'd gone off in a car with a man in a blue suit. It was even suggested that relatives of the boy, living in the South Shields area, had whisked him away, but this at least proved to be untrue.

The appearance of the clairvoyant, a Mrs. Pearce, gave Annie Smith fresh hope, for she told Annie that the boy was not far from home, and that his disappearance was connected with a boy of some twelve years or so. Annie believed her, to the extent that she went to the police and recounted what she'd heard, and the Detective in charge set up a search in the area of Unicorn street and North Street, his men searching from house to house, all the time drawing closer to Orange Street.

It was not until September that the truth finally came to light. James Kearigan, a Dockyard labourer, lived only yards away from Annie Smith, at 55 Orange Street. He was a widower, sharing a home with his mother and fourteen-year-old son Leonard. The boy had been in the Infirmary for some time (since the week after Georgie's disappearance, in fact) following a serious epileptic fit, and on the afternoon of Sunday 3 September, James Kearigan had visited him in the Infirmary, later stopping on the way home to spend some time at his wife's graveside.

Back at the house, he had decided to look out an old pair of trousers which he remembered were kept in a box in the attic. The box was under an old bed, almost hidden from view by an assortment of unwanted clothing, curtains and other bits of cloth.

He opened the box. Later, he told the police, 'I turned the clothing over inside, and came across what appeared to be a dolly or a dummy, which had been apparently clothed by a child for amusement. I took hold of the little arm, and was shocked to find it was a human body'.

Shocked by his discovery, he had run to the police, and the rest of that day was a patchwork of questions and cross-questions. No, he said, he'd had no suspicion of anything awry in the house, he accepted that it was possible someone could have entered the house while he was at work and, yes, they could have done it without his mother hearing, and he agreed that his son sometimes brought children back to the house to play. But beyond that . . .

Little Georgie had been bound with a rope and covered with old clothing, but he had been dead for so long that it was difficult to tell just how he had died. The two doctors conducting the post mortem eventually come to the conclusion that the poor child was still alive when he had been put in the box. Further details, too gruesome to list, led the police to focus their attention on young Lennie.

On two separate occasions Lennie was taken to the Town Hall police station for questioning, but it was clear that he genuinely knew nothing about Georgie's death. However, during the time he was in police custody, he appeared to suffer further attacks of epilepsy, coming to to give vivid accounts of the dreams he had had - dreams which amounted to nothing less than an involuntary confession of his guilt.

> In his dream Leonard met little Georgie Smith in the street. The little boy had some sweets in a piece of paper. They had made him thirsty and he asked Leonard for a drink . . . so in his dream, Leonard took Georgie to his house.
>
> 'I showed him into our kitchen,' said Leonard. 'Then I put him on my back and carried him upstairs. Then I put him in the box and covered him up with some old clothes, and shut the lid down'. . . .
>
> 'I didn't know I had done it until last night I had the dream,

and it came to me.'[10]

Later he was to recount another dream, in which he had tied up the little boy when he was still alive. 'He must have died from suffocation because he could not get the lid off'.

It was obvious that, awake and fully conscious, he knew nothing of Georgie's death. Nevertheless, on Tuesday 5 September he was charged with murder. On 9 September, the second day of the inquest, the story was made yet more distressing when the Coroner observed that, had he lived, Georgie would have been four years old that very day.

The inquest was adjourned until 19 September, when the Doctor was finally able to offer an explanation for the mystery that surrounded the murder. In his considered opinion:

> In major epilepsy . . . just after or just before a fit, a person might commit criminal acts of which he has no memory at a later date, and for which he was not responsible.

The Coroner sought to clarify this statement so that the jury should be in no doubt:

> If the jury were satisfied that the boy was responsible for putting the deceased into the box, then he would advise that the jury could not assume that he put him there innocently. If he put him there under a condition of epilepsy, the responsibility was not theirs, but for another Court to deal with.

The jury's verdict was 'that he (Georgie) was put into the box alive', but that Leonard Kearigan was 'not mentally responsible for his actions at the time'; accordingly the fourteen-year-old boy, Leonard Kearigan, was remanded to appear before the Hampshire Assizes in the following November.

At the trial he pleaded Not Guilty, but with the evidence to hand the jury were out for less than three minutes, to return a verdict of 'Guilty but at the time of the act insane'. Inevitably, Mr. Justice Horridge sentenced Leonard to be kept in custody as a criminal lunatic 'until his Majesty's pleasure be known' – adding, more kindly, 'Of course, the boy will be taken away and cared for'.[11]

Brighton Mary

Less than six months after the death of little Georgie Smith, and a bare stone's throw from his home, a prostitute was murdered in her bed.

The story of Mary Pelham[12] has its place in Portsea's history, not so much because it concerns the death of a prostitute but because the setting for the crime – Blossom Alley – shocked public opinion out of its customary complacency, resulting in a call for slum clearance that would have been difficult to ignore. It was estimated at the time that some 20,000 people lived in the appalling conditions that existed in the courts and alleys off Queen Street and in the equally notorious Voller Street area of Landport.

Only days after the murder, an article appeared in the *Evening News* describing the full horrors of Blossom Alley, and this brought a response from one reader that personified the feelings of many:

> We as citizens should do our duty and protect against such hovels and slums being allowed to exist. We, as good citizens, should protest against any proposals . . . to embellish or beautify Portsmouth or Southsea while such places as Blossom Alley, Voller Street etc., are allowed to remain as they are

But however much conscience deplored the situation, it was to take six years for work to be started on this particular slum area, and it is sobering to think that even after World War 2 there were still plans in hand for the work to be completed. And it all began with the murder of 'Brighton Mary'.

Mary Frances Pelham came from the North of England, married to a Herman Pelham whom she had met while in domestic service in Sunderland. When her husband went off to war, she came south, first to Brighton and later to Portsmouth, where she set up home in No.14 Blossom Alley. When Herman came back from the war, he already knew her to be a prostitute, but he was so dismayed by the squalor of the life she was leading that he turned on his heel and left her forever.

Many of the prostitutes were well liked, they were kind to the children that lived thereabouts, and, if anyone were in need, they were free with whatever food or money they had to spare. Mary Pelham was no exception; not only was she a good neighbour, she was equally well-known for her generosity to a sailor in trouble, taking him home, feeding him and letting him 'sleep it off' if he were the worse for drink - anything to keep him safe from Naval patrols. Someone was heard to describe her as 'a mother to the matelots, as well as a woman', and this would seem to be a fair comment.

On the night she died, Mary Pelham was seen arm-in-arm with a sailor, apparently heading for home. Fifteen minutes later she reappeared in Queen Street, making her way to a restaurant, the *'Live and Let Live'*, where she went up to the counter and demanded food for her kitten. 'I'm in a hurry,' she said. 'I've got to get some chips for my chap at home'.

Next morning, her neighbour Mary Riley was passing No.14 when she noticed the door was open. She called to her friend, but there was no answer so she went inside. Puzzled by the silence, she climbed the stairs to Mary's bedroom and opened the door.

Mary lay on the bed, dead, the victim of an appalling attack:

> Around the head and shoulders the bedclothes were darkened in a sticky mass of blood. A gash, from Mary Pelham's forehead to the top of her nose, glistened in the light. Tied, in a half-hitch, around her neck was a light blue handkerchief or scarf. On the bed, the shattered parts of a pint oat malt stout bottle.

Detectives from Scotland Yard was called to the scene, while local police, given a tip-off, turned their attention to a sailor aboard the battleship *Ramilles*. He was taken for questioning but he was never formally arrested, nor indeed was his name ever released to the public.

Neighbours were unable to help; they could have been expected to hear the sound of the the man's boots on the cobblestones as he ran away, for Blossom Alley echoed every footstep, but they had heard nothing, and it was assumed that he must have made his escape barefoot.

There was only the light blue scarf, 'tied in a half-hitch', and a ticket for 'Cabin 220' at the Royal Sailors' Rest, found near the body, to suggest the crime was committed by a sailor; but with nothing more to go on, the mystery remained unsolved, to be buried for all time by the demolition that was to follow years later.

PART VII

'LITTLE WORLDS OF TROUBLE AND DISASTER'

In a newspaper article published on 10 October 1866, there is a report on several of the charities in existence at the time. One of these concerned Thomas Fitzherbert who, in his will dated 8 June 1821, left £10,000 in 4% Bank annuities:

> the dividends to be for the benefit of maintenance of five poor men, married or single, ten poor widows, and five poor single women, of the age fifty years, or upwards, born within the guildable part of Portsea, and resident in the parish at the time of their election, and shall have resided at least ten years previous.[1]

Exactly one hundred years later, in 1921, the Crown Prince of Japan paid a formal visit to Portsmouth, at the end of which he donated the sum of £1,000 for local charities. In the years between there was a constant need for support of the poor over and above the help available from the workhouse and by such educational institutions as the Beneficial Society School, the Free Ragged Schools and the Seamen and Marines' Orphans School. This gap was filled to some extent by such provision for the poor as the Eltham Charity – a sum of £3,000, the income of which was to be distributed amongst 'poor persons residing within certain districts of the Borough', and similarly the Winter and Mills Charities and that of Thomas King, though the latter added the note that 'No person is eligible who has been convicted of drunkenness'. More effective, perhaps, were the activities of the various voluntary organisations.

One of these, the Portsmouth and Portsea Ladies' Benevolent Society was to have a far more lasting effect than its founders could possibly have imagined. Initially, the Society's aim was:

> to lessen those evils to which the wives, children, and widows of sailors and soldiers are peculiarly subject, and to assist

those who are at a distance from their parishes to return home, and, if funds permit, to give help to other sick persons and poor married women in their lyings-in.[2]

Founded in January 1807, in its first year alone the Society was to offer assistance to nearly seven hundred people in need; this figure rose in the next three years to over a thousand, and the Society continued to function with varying degrees of success until 1928 when it was disbanded. It has been claimed, however, that its members' contribution to the welfare of the people formed the basis of the present-day hospital service in the City.

Trading under an equally ponderous title, The Portsmouth Rescue Society and Protestant Home for Fallen Women[3] was based in Hyde Park Road, but it was to the Mission Room at 2, Marylebone Road in Southsea that these 'fallen women' were sent initially, to await despatch to the local Home or to the Female Preventive and Reformatory Institution in London.

Rehabilitation was available for any who were 'desirous of leaving Portsmouth and getting their old associations both out of sight and out of memory'; but the women were expected to make some contribution to the running of the Home, and there was always work for them in the Home Laundry, the main source of the Home's income. However, in an Annual Report issued by the Society in 1894, there is a note about a Restaurant situated at one corner of the premises, which was let to Messrs. Shepherd and Son, the Railway carriers, and more surprisingly:

the Private Hotel, with its Coffee Room and eight Beds, (which) is still carried on by the staff of the Home, and promises to contribute a substantial channel of income to the Institution.

The Report was brief and dealt principally with the death of the Superintendent, Mrs. Colebrook, but it also gives some figures for the previous year, showing what had become of the women in the Society's care:

Sent into service	17
Sent home to friends	26
Left at own request	22
Sent to Union Hospital	8
Sent to Lock Hospital	5
Sent to our own refuge	8
Scaled the wall at night time	1
Died in the Home	1
Remained in the Home	121.

What, one wonders, became of the poor soul driven to 'scale the wall at night time' . . . ?

If these 'fallen women' were not to turn to the Portsmouth Rescue Society there was still the Salvation Army, for it was at the Army's Rescue Home in Nobbs Lane that 'the Women and girls taken from the streets are housed and fed, and work is provided for them in the laundry attached to the Home'.

In the 1880s, the mission work of the Salvation Army extended far beyond the prostitute, embracing as it did all manner of men and women in need; in spite of considerable opposition it went ahead with the provision of a Home for one hundred Naval and Military men to stay when they were free from duty, followed by the opening of two reception centres, one in Southsea and one in North Street, Portsea. And it was the Salvation Army that provided the 'Farthing Breakfasts' at their centre near Bonfire Corner.

Free Breakfasts

Long before the Education (Provision of Meals) Act of 1906, teachers in the town had been aware that there were children in their care who were little short of starving, and in 1890 they had joined forces to provide the poorest children with a breakfast of cocoa, bread and jam. This was a valuable enough gesture at any time, but particularly so in the winter that followed, when the town was to suffer the most severe weather for some eighty years. To give them a degree of resistance to the elements, all Board School children were provided with free breakfasts throughout the eight weeks of freezing frost.[4]

The local Press heard of this enterprise and, in a fine-gesture of support, launched an appeal for funds that resulted in the formation of the 'Free Breakfast Committee', offering a breakfast in most of the schools throughout the following winter. This undertaking continued to operate for several years until it was replaced by official Government provision of food under the 1906 Act; seven feeding centres were set up, including one at the St. George's Institute in St. George's Square, and the menus prepared were common to all centres, and once established remained almost unchanged well into the 1940s.

Parents had to apply for free meals, supplying some evidence of hardship, but in the case of a child suffering from serious malnutrition, the Authority would arrange for free meals to be supplied, with or without parental consent, the money to be recouped from the parents if possible.

Between the start of the scheme in 1909 and 1914 there was an amazing improvement in the general state of health among schoolchildren. And whereas meals had originally been provided in term-time only, in 1913 free meals were continued throughout the school holiday periods. Two years after the war, the Schools Canteen Committee tackled the question of supplying breakfasts as well as midday meals, and in support of this the Schools Medical Officer arranged for several of the poorer children to be examined. This revealed that over 50% were 'in a state of sub-normal nutrition' and 50% were inadequately clothed. It was also remarked that 50% were fatherless . . .

The Brotherhood Boot Fund

In 1910 the *Evening News* arranged for 2000 children to be entertained and clothed at Christmas time, using funds collected by *News* staff and their relatives. After the event was over, it was discovered that £50 still remained in hand, and with this money the organisers agreed to purchase boots for all the children 'who came bootless to the feast'.

This kind gesture has been recognised as the beginning of the 'Boot Fund', which the *News* organised for many years until it was taken over by the local benevolent society, the 'Portsmouth Brotherhood'.[5]

There were strict rules for people applying to the Brotherhood Boot Fund; applicants had to complete a form which made it quite clear that the boots did not come as a gift but rather as a loan. Furthermore, the parent in question was liable to undertake minor repairs, and to return the boots if required so to do. They had also to agree not to pawn them or sell the boots - and to ensure that a pair of Boot Fund boots would not walk too far afield, Rule 7 (of 18) specified 'All boots and shoes to be stamped P.B.B.F.'

Children up to school-leaving age were eligible to receive suitable footwear, but – as the Fund's Revised Standing Orders of April 1935 indicate – a child could expect 'One pair of boots or shoes only during the season. Not more than two pairs to any family'. There were, in fact, some exceptions to this in the case of a large family.

The Workshop for the Blind made a considerable contribution to the Fund's activities, producing warm stockings for the winter which the Brotherhood purchased from them and handed out to special deserving cases. 'Two pairs (of socks or stockings) may be supplied to each pair of Boots issued to children of Widows, deserted Women or any Necessitous Cases of large families' (Rule 12).

Only pride prevented a mother going to the Boot Fund for assistance and she would do all she could to delay the inevitable, offering any excuse to explain her need, pleading illness in the family, or a sudden bereavement; perhaps it was the unseasonal cold weather that had caught the children without suitable footwear – any tale would do rather than reveal the despair that unemployment brought to what the Brotherhood called their 'little worlds of trouble and disaster'.

The Brotherhood Boot Fund had many allies – the SPCK, School Attendance Officers, the Society of St. Vincent de Paul and the Toc-H;

Portsmouth Brotherhood

Life President : W. R. WARD　　　　　　　　　　**President : E. ADAMS**

Motto : "DEEDS, NOT WORDS."

(INCORPORATING COSHAM AND DISTRICT)

BOOT FUND
1936　　　　　　　　1937

"Inasmuch as ye have done it unto one of these the least of My children ye have done it unto Me."

The Portsmouth Brotherhood Boot Fund Committee

appeal to you on this, the 26th year of the fund, for your generous support in this great effort on behalf of the poor kiddies, so that there shall not be one deserving kiddie in Portsmouth without boots.

Impostors are prosecuted.

Every case is carefully investigated.

There is no religious or political distinction.

Last winter 1,863 pairs of boots were issued. Total boots issued to date is over 40,802 pairs. Already issued this season, 1,275 pairs. The boots are repaired by our Blind Brothers. Surgical boots for children are also provided. The Brotherhood accounts are audited by the City Treasurer. The whole of the work is done gratuitously by Brotherhood Members. If you should mislay the envelope you may place your contribution in the box loose, or you can ask the collector for another envelope.

BOOT FUND COMMITTEE :

Chairman　　-　　Mr. J. G. HAMILTON.

Hon. Secretary : Eng. Lieut. Com. J. Lippiett, R.N., 34 Derby Road, North End.

Hon. Organising Secretary : W. E. Beabey, 103 Locksway Road, Southsea.

Hon. Financial Secretary : Captain C. T. Savill, R.M., 55 Linden Road, Alverstoke, Gosport, to whom all Donations should be sent.

PLEASE NOTE.—Only persons wearing the Red Collar Badges are Official Collectors. All boxes are sealed and marked with the Brotherhood Stamp.

PLEASE HELP THE KIDDIES!

In the event of the envelope not being collected, you are kindly requested to return it to the Hon. Fin. Sec., Captain C. T. Savill, R.M., 55 Linden Road, Alverstoke, Gosport.

These handbills are printed without charge to the above association by

BOOTS PURE DRUG CO. LIMITED, NOTTINGHAM.

Portsmouth Brotherhood Boot Fund Committee Appeal, 1936-1937.
(PCRO 449A/2)

and in 1936 the Lord Mayor's Charity fund, distributing a total of £520 to various good causes, gave ten guineas to the Boot Fund.

The Rev. F.W.Rumsby

The Rev. Mr. F.W. Rumsby was never to receive the public acclaim of such well-known figures as Father Dolling, but in his quiet way he was to make an equally valuable contribution to the wellbeing of the people of Portsea.

In the early 1920s, he and his wife decided to give up their living in an elegant residential part of London to come to the Kent Street Baptist Church in Portsea.[6] He was as shocked by local conditions as any benefactor before him, and he immediately began to campaign against the dreadful surroundings he found there. By starting with the poor housing that still existed after the first War, he and Mrs. Rumsby were largely responsible for the formation of Portsmouth Housing Ltd., aimed at persuading the better-off in the Borough to contribute toward a scheme that would result eventually in the building of the Hawke Street flats.

Mrs. Rumsby involved herself in the pastoral side of the scheme; it was she who attended to the running of the flats, collected the rents and made a point of keeping in touch with the residents so that she could offer advice and comfort where the need arose. Being something of a poet and an artist, she contributed much of her artistic work to charity bazaars to raise funds for those in real distress, and both she and her husband worked constantly to persuade the better-off to spare a shilling or two toward the help of the elderly. They ran a Second-Hand Clothes Room which flourished, and they collected books and toys for the children; but always desperate for funds, Mr. Rumsby was to give voice more than once to his opinion that if he could only lay his hands on £500 a year he would be able to distribute small sums around the parish where the need was greatest. No one, he claimed, knew better than he where the real poverty lay.

'Miss Robinson'

There are two individuals whose names stand out vividly, remarkable for their determination and success in the face of personal and, on occasions, civic discouragement.

The first of these was Sarah Robinson, 'somewhat imperious, but with a heart of gold'. She was a confirmed teetotaller, campaigning vigorously for the rescue of soldiers and sailors from the hazards of Portsmouth in general and the Dockyard area in particular:

> *Thursday, June 16th.* (1870) Mr. T.B.Smithies gave a tea-meeting at the Beneficial Society's Hall, Portsea, to the teetotallers

of the Channel Squadron . . . Mr. Gregson went on H.M.S. 'MINOTAUR', the flag-ship, to ask leave of Captain Goodenough for this, and he had the men marched to it amid the laughter and jeers of the Portsea roughs.[7]

And in the following year, with a touch of humour she notes in her journal, *'Portsmouth* – Another big Tea for sailors given today by Mr. T.B. Smithies . . . no one was *marched* here this time . . .

It is in this same entry that she refers to her colleague - or rival - Agnes Weston:

> One of the Sergeants . . . bragged a little about Miss Robinson being the Soldiers' Friend . . . when up jumped a fine bluejacket and said *they* had a lady too, Miss Weston of Bath.

In her book, *A Life Record*, she made frequent reference to Agnes Weston, and in 1873 they actually met. Rivalry there probably was, and certainly Sarah Robinson admired her counterpart even while there was a hint of envy for her success: 'How little I imagined that in 1876 Miss Weston would establish that splendid Sailors' Rest' (at the gates of Devonport Dockyard).

In any event, there was room for both women, Miss Robinson opening the substantial Soldiers' and Sailors' Institute in the High Street, and a 'small place' in Camden Alley in 1897, which proved 'worse than useless' because of its limited accommodation, followed by the 'Sailors' Welcome' in Queen Street. The intention was to give the service men somewhere respectable to pass their free time, but unfortunately her efforts met with much abuse from the ruder elements of the crowd, a fact which she refers to more than once in her Journal:

> When we went to the Dockyard to meet any troopship we had to pass through a mob of land sharks and women, who cursed me for 'spoiling sport' and 'taking the bread out of other people's mouths'. Mud was often thrown into my cab, our windows were broken, door-mats cut up, disgusting anonymous letters sent, and people would bawl after soldiers in the street, asking if they were some of Miss Robinson's lambs.

'Aggie Weston'

The early years of Agnes Weston's life gave no clue to the career she would choose for herself once she had broken away from strong family influence. Her parents were respectable and God-loving, her mother something of an invalid, who had been advised to move from London to the cleaner air of Bath, and it was there that the children spent a happy and totally conventional Victorian childhood.

Through a friend, a Miss Williams, she became involved in temperance meetings, held in the worst parts of Bath where the evils of drink were all too obvious. It was at one of these meetings that she was challenged and had to admit that she was not a teetotaller:

> It was an awful moment; what could I do, what could I say?... the audience as well as the man waited for my reply. I had to say, "No, I am not exactly a teetotaller, but I only take a glass of wine occasionally." "Right you are," answered my tormentor; "that's exactly what I do; I take a glass sometimes for the benefit of my health." . . . and, throwing down the pen, he shouldered his way out of the room.[8]

She was bitterly ashamed of her part in the incident and it proved to be a turning point in her life, for she developed a passionate dislike for alcohol and its effects. Determined to campaign against such evil, she needed all the personality she could muster, first to persuade individuals and organisations to support her financially, and secondly, to convince soldiers and sailors alike that they were better off accepting the warmth of her 'family' meetings than spending their time in pubs and brothels. It was a fearsome task, often it looked as though she must fail, and she owed much of her success to the support of her great friend, Sophia Wintz.

The Sailors' Rest in Portsmouth began as a coffee bar and reading-room in the Music-Hall in Commercial Road. Although Agnes Weston was seeking to do the work of God, she was not averse to a bit of singing and dancing, recitations and 'feats of agility and strength' – always provided that the entertainment was of a seemly and respectable nature. The venture proved an immense success, and in the course of time sufficient funds had been raised to build more suitable premises. In June 1881 the Portsmouth Sailors' Rest was formally opened.

Not surprisingly, those publicans based close to the Dockyard gate were less than pleased with the way Agnes Weston was enticing their customers away from the 'dens of iniquity' that remained open till well into the night. One of her contemporaries, commenting on a remark in Agnes Weston's Annual Report that 'cash takings over the counter amounted to £33,204 19s. 3d.', wrote:

> . . . temperance workers would have good cause to thank Almighty God for the practical temperance results of such a counter-attraction to the public houses. A very considerable portion of that £33,000 has been saved from the public-house till.

But Agnes Weston was offering the sailors more than hospitality: she wrote letters for them and accepted the role of banker when they asked her to mind their money. In 1878, at the time of the sinking of the *Eurydice*, she visited many of the bereaved families, shocked to see the appalling living conditions in the Dockyard area; and later she turned her attention to the many wives and widows who suffered great hardship because of the Admiralty ruling over pay for dependents. During the winter of 1914-15 she took it upon herself to collect vast supplies of warm clothing for her 'bluejackets' in the North Sea and the 'soldiers in France and Flanders, who stood up to their waists in half-frozen waters in the trenches'. By the turn of the century she was able to write that 'if our Royal Sailors' Rests have done nothing else, they demonstrate clearly that the bluejacket of the twentieth century does not need the attractions of strong drink', and in 1908 she received a letter from Sandringham, 'by command of the King':

> to say that nobody is better aware of, nor more thoroughly appreciates, the great work you have done for the British sailor, and for their wives and children also, than His Majesty is, and he thanks you sincerely for the same.

She died suddenly in 1918, but her work continued, thanks mainly to the efforts of Sophia Wintz, and after the Second World War the Trustees of the Rests came to the decision that there was still a place for the work begun by Agnes Weston – by the early 1950's the new Portsmouth Rest was open for business, to be followed by others, even as far afield as Singapore.

There were many messages of sympathy at the time of her death, but probably that of her friend, Lord Charles Beresford, best summed up the feelings of everyone who had come in contact with her:

> The whole Navy appreciated her untiring energy, her chivalrous and unselfish work in trying to benefit the men on the lower deck. I have lost an affectionate friend, but the good she has done will live after. . .

'Brother Bob'

The story of local conditions in the 19th century would not be complete without mentioning the work of Robert Radclyffe Dolling, *Father* Dolling – or 'Brother Bob' as he was known to many of the people he gathered around him.

Described as a 'rotund Irishman with the heavy cheeks and kind, wise eyes', he was Priest-in-Charge of the Winchester College Mission at St. Agatha's, Landport from 1885-1896, and he wrote about his experiences

in a book he called *Ten Years in a Portsmouth Slum*[9]. His rather fulsome
style of writing makes it difficult to take an objective view of the good
he did during that period, but the book suggests that this was not only
a history of his ten years at St. Agatha's, but more particularly his
defence against the case made by the Bishop, who firmly rejected his
'high church' method of ministering to his flock.

His fellow workers, and even more his parishioners, thought the
world of him, and whatever impression he gives the present-day reader,
it would be foolish to ignore what he has to say in a book full of
first-hand knowledge of the poor and their problems. The fact that he
served for three years on the School Board, and for a time on the Board
of Guardians would have given him considerable insight into conditions, and his personal contact with the people gives a vivid picture of
life in his parish. He talked of 'all the sin, poverty, and squalor of
S. Agatha's district . . of which every house had been built a hundred
years ago', and at one point he described the scene in Charlotte Street:

> . . .from end to end, an open fair; cheapjacks screaming;
> laughing crowds round them, never seeming to buy ; women,
> straggling under the weight of a baby, trying to get the sunday
> dinner a little cheaper because things had begun to get stale;
> great louts of lads standing at the corners. . . slatternly
> women creeping out of some little public house . . .[10]

He talked of 'this poor little district, with its eleven hundred little
houses and its fifty-two public houses'; he referred with anguish to the
number of public houses in relation to the number of people, no less to
the brothels, the 'bad houses' as he calls them.

Perhaps he is entitled to boast that by his persistence and his
harrying of the landlords, (combined with the help of the Superintendent of Police and the School Board Officer), he could claim to have
cleared out all the Landport brothels, the 'plague spots', until, just
before he left in 1896, he 'bought for £250 the only bad house remaining'

On his arrival he had taken his cue from his predecessor, Dr. Link-
later, who, in his time had aimed for three major targets: a free school
for the children of the parish, a high school for 'those of a better class',
and above all a sense of social obligation that would bring the community into one Christian family. He had gone a long way toward
achieving these aims, but Father Dolling was more than a little daunted
when he saw what remained to be done, and at one stage suggested that
had he known the task that lay ahead of him, he might well have
withdrawn right at the start.

He began his work at St. Agatha's with what he called his 'Gymnasium', set up in a disused chapel in Clarence Street which, with a Sunday
School room, a caretaker's house and other small buildings purchased

for something over £3,000 – money he raised as much by faith as with the assistance of an understanding bank.

He had inherited several independent youth clubs from his predecessor, rough, lawless and each exclusive to themselves; but he was determined to bring them together under one roof, not least for reasons of economy, and in an effort to keep things simple, he laid down just four house rules: no gambling, no bad language, no losing of temper, no annoying anyone else – rules which were frequently flouted by undisciplined youths who frequented the clubs.

The volunteers who came to help in the Gymnasium frequently went through some rough handling as a result of their well-meant effort, and partly in despair, but not without humour, Father Dolling wrote:

> I have seen them skilfully lassoed, arms and legs bound, and lashed to the gymnasium ladder . . . I have seen them spread-eagled upon the vaulting horse, with a dance of savage Indians whooping around them.

And of the equipment, so dearly gathered together:

> I have seen all the mattresses ripped up and kicked to pieces. . . the bagatelle-tables used as points of vantage, from which opposing forces sprang at each other. I have seen men playing upon the piano with their feet, and I have known . . . the fierce joy of tearing away the front of the piano, and strewing the broken hammers artistically on the floor.[11]

But even in the midst of this devastation the good man is confident that such louts can change their ways; given a lead and a target to aim for, reformation is perfectly possible for such 'mean and unambitious people quivering with the passion of daring to achieve success'.

He frequently showed a touching naiveté as for instance when he preached in London on the subject of sailors, expressing his view that Portsmouth, in common with most naval towns, was a sink of iniquity. 'I was utterly astonished when I arrived at the railway station, on my return, to discover the extraordinary storm my words had created'.

Not surprisingly, the Mayor sprang to the defence of his town, concerned no doubt for the welfare of hotels, guests houses and shopkeepers. To refute Father Dolling's observation, he claimed to have visited fifty back-street public houses and beerhouses, 'between the hours of 9.40 and 11.00 p.m', and declared himself satisfied that he had done a serious statistical study of the people seen at this time.

'Do not let it go forth,' he said, 'that I just opened the door and looked in', and in a final burst of indignation he demanded to know whether Father Dolling's sermon was preached to raise money for the proposed new church – and if so, 'I should be sorry to go and pray in a church built from money raised by stigmatising a town as this clergyman has done'.[12]

Among his reactions to this diatribe, Father Dolling artfully posed the question whether, in a period of just eighty minutes one single person could even manage to enter fifty public houses, never mind thoroughly study them for character and decorum.

For all the good he was doing, Father Dolling had been at the Mission only two years when petitions began to appear on the desk of the Bishop of Winchester, who wrote to him on one occasion about 'paragraphs and letters in various newspapers about your proceedings at St. Agatha's . . .I am told that your own people generally, though attached to you, would prefer a less pronounced ritual'. In 1889, he was asked whether he would be willing to give up certain practices, among them, the use of incense at Celebrations, Service of Compline ('at which, as far as I can gather, the choir practically absolve the priest'), and Vespers for the Dead.[13]

This was the beginning of a protracted dispute which was to end seven years later with Father Dolling's resignation, but in the meantime he was adamant in his conviction that he was doing what was right for his congregation and he had no intention of changing his ways.

Such faith and such optimism deserved to win, and by the end of his ten years, Father Dolling not only had the lasting affection and respect of most of his parish, he could congratulate himself on such concrete evidence of success as 'the wonderful Gymnasium, the parsonage, the day-schools, the almshouses, the Mission-house, old S. Agatha's, and new S. Agatha's, nearly all of which had been built by my begging'. On 24 March 1891, Father Dolling reported to his subscribers on the results of the past five years:

> We have put into the army 39 young men, into the navy 57 young men. We have emigrated to Australia, America and elesewhere 63. We have started in life over 100 young men who lived with us. We have reformed 25 thieves just out of gaol. We have sent to service and into shops about 100 girls. 25 girls have passed through our training Home for from two to five years . . . We have turned many drunkards into self-respecting, church-going people. We have rescued 144 fallen women . . . We have maintained, and are maintaining in preventive Homes 124 children, snatched from the brink of ruin. We have shut up in the district over 50 brothels . . . We feed for a halfpenny a meal 180 children, and 25 old people free, twice a week during the winter. We teach over 500 children in our Sunday Schools, and 600 in our Day

Typical activities at St. Agatha's – 'The Cleaning Party'… c.1910.
(Mr. F.J. Green's collection at PCRO. 1483A/3/5/18)

… and the 'Lady Morris Dancers', c.1911.
(Mr. F.J. Green's collection at PCRO)

schools . . . We have an acrobatic troupe, dancing class, and glee club; a sewing club; a large temperance society, and Band of Hope; a lending library, and three penny savings banks'.[14]

With some justification Father Dolling ended his book with a bitter reference to the Bishop:

I wonder if any thought passed through his mind that he was actually, at that moment, killing the goose that had laid the golden eggs – truly a goose, for was it wise to lay out ten years of one's life in effecting all this . . .?[15]

'Brother Bob'

PART VIII

'THE BAND WILL PLAY . . .'

For the rich there is always some form of recreation available, and even the modestly well-off will buy a ticket for the theatre or the football match, but the poor must very largely seek their own amusement.

In 19th century Portsea this would generally mean going to the public-house, where there would be not only food and drink on offer, but also some form of live entertainment, for at that time the music hall was most often lodged in the same premises as the public-house.

Some of these music halls were perfectly respectable, but others – like the one in Military Row – would attract off-duty soldiers or recently 'paid-off' seamen with money to burn, and the evening could well end in brawling and general disorder.

By contrast, the 'smoking concert' was popular with service men, often a perfectly decorous and well conducted affair that marked those present as gentlemen who gave every indication that they knew how things should be done. One such event took place in October 1896:

> The 5th Co. R.E. held a smoking concert last evening at the Three Crowns, Portsea, to give a "send-off" to a draft of their comrades who left this morning for service abroad. Corporal Blake was in the chair, and Miss Tatford presided at the piano. Sappers Gamble, Thompson, North, Jones, Amour, Lance-Corporals Hands and Conneston, and Bugler Dixon contributed some admirable songs. At 11.30 the merry party broke up with the singing of "Auld Lang Syne".[1]

There was at one time nowhere else for them to go. There was no alternative to back-street lodgings and the vulgar entertainment to be found there until funds were raised in support of a project to build the Royal Sailors' Home in Queen Street. It was opened on St. George's Day, 1851, and proved popular with the men for whom it was designed, and also met with Royal approval, for Queen Victoria was

The Band of the Royal Marines, The Hard – pre-First World War.
(Portsmouth Polytechnic Central Photography Unit)

… the young would have continued their games on street corners…'
(By courtesy of The News, Portsmouth)

persuaded to contribute £100 toward the fund.[2]

In an attempt to improve upon the situation overall, a move was made to restrict the opening hours of licensed premises, based on the idea that 'no house should be opened between one and four o'clock in the morning' . . .. At the first hearing this modest restriction was soundly defeated, though at a special meeting of the Town Council in 1866, members were finally persuaded to come round to the idea, adopting the Public House Act brought into force two years before.

Apart from the public houses and the Victoria Music Hall in North Street, indoor entertainment was confined to such places as the Beneficial Hall and St. George's Hall in the Square; both of these offered accommodation for public gatherings, and sometimes Charles Dickens himself would be present to give one of his 'readings'. In the 1870s onwards, song recitals and political meetings took place at the Portland Hall, and there was the Grand Palace in Gunwharf Road, the Theatre Royal in Commercial Road, and the Prince's Theatre in Lake Road; but such pleasures as an evening at the theatre or at the Esplanade Assembly Rooms were unlikely to feature in the lives of many Portsea people at that time, for it cost good money to get in. More readily available – and possibly more enjoyable – would have been a visit from a foreign ship, or from royalty making a tour of the town, when everyone would drop what they were doing, to line the streets and cheer, glad to have something to cheer about. In 1887, Golden Jubilee Year, festivities had included a splendid review of the troops on Southsea Common, 23,000 children were invited to take part in a special celebration, and a whole bullock had been roasted at Landport, to feed the poor people of the town.

In more modern times, one such occasion marked the visit of King Edward VIII, when the people of Portsea turned out with great enthusiasm to greet him as he drove along the Hard. He was to become the first Freeman of the City, and liked to make reference to 'his' Navy, little knowing that within six months of that initial visit, he would come back again, for the last time . . .

The 1937 Coronation provided as much free entertainment as anyone could wish; there was a torchlight procession, with music from the Band of the Royal Marines, there were tree-planting ceremonies on Portsdown Hill, street parties with fireworks displays, beacons were lit and there was a tattoo at Fratton Park that proved immensely popular. Thirty-five thousand school children were presented with Coronation mugs and they were invited to a free cinema show to see the Coronation on film, an opportunity extended to many pensioners, who also received a celebration half-a-crown.

The festivities were to continue, with a Royal Review of the Fleet in May, while the Lord Mayor 'showed hospitality to all classes of people in the City', holding a party in the Guildhall every Saturday evening for some weeks, to which Service and ex-Service men were invited, together with Corporation workmen, Dockyard employees, Civil Servants and others.

Any such outdoor event was likely to draw a vast audience, if only because the entertainment was free . Thus, for many years Guy Fawkes Day was celebrated with a great gathering of people at Bonfire Corner, the Mayor was invited to join in, and later there would be a banquet in honour of the occasion. People gathered to hear Regimental Bands concerts, and the Point Regatta invariably drew such a huge crowd that the authorities were obliged to close the harbour for the duration of the event, for fear of running down one of the numerous small boats that milled around in the water.

The Free Mart Fair had been held ever since the Charter was granted in the twelfth century, 'to be free to all people, natives and foreigners, free from tolls, duties impositions &c., and no one to be arrested for debt, or oppressed in any way during its continuance'. In the early days it had been, as with most fairs, a market place for the sale of woollen cloth, pots and cutlery from all over the country, not to mention such items as metal ware from Holland and baskets from Normandy. It was an opportunity for the housewife to stock up on domestic bits and pieces, to meet far-distant family and friends she was unlikely to see again till the following year, for people from all the county would do their best to be there if it could possibly be managed.

Mostly, they came with a purpose and the side shows were little more than diversion from the real business in hand; but with the arrival of the railway people could travel more freely, there was no longer a need for a commercial focal point in any one area, and the market element of the Free Mart Fair began to give way to the amusement side.

The Penny Peep Show was there, the Fat Lady, the Dwarf and the Albinos, and at the Crown Hotel, Signor Bertolotto's 'exhibition of industrious Fleas':

> . . . patronised by Her Royal Highness the Princess Augusta, their Majesties the King and Queen of the French, the King and Queen of the Belgians, the nobility and gentry, &c. . . . where you may see fleas harnessed drawing coaches, tandems, fighting duels, personating Waterloo heroes, manning a ship of war, &c, . . .

All this, plus a history of the flea by Signor Bertolotto, was available for the price of One Shilling, for the annual fourteen-day period of the Free Mart Fair. But with the change in its function, so the spirit of the Fair degenerated to one of drunken rowdiness and petty crime, until it became obvious that it could not continue and in 1846 it was finally closed down by an Act of Parliament.[3]

The Portsdown Fair was little more than a three-day extension of the Free Mart Fair, the stall-holders and entertainers moving on to the top of Portsdown Hill to continue the revelry, but this soon deteriorated in the same way as its predecessor, to be closed down in 1861. There was a last attempt to revitalise the Fair in Cosham Park, and though it was as popular as ever, people crowding there by special train, by horse-drawn cab, by any means available, the drunk and disorderly element was soon to spoil the event yet again, and it too had to be abandoned.

However, it was beginning to become apparent that spending time out of doors was not only a pleasurable form of recreation, it was also very good for the health; in consequence, moves were made to purchase land to turn into parks, gardens and recreation grounds. In 1875 the Government offered a part of Lump's Fort as recreation ground, and three years later, the persistence of Alderman Emanuel Emanuel and several colleagues was rewarded when the War Office agreed to to release part of the Portsea fortifications for development as a 'People's Park'. The destruction of the 'grand old elm trees' which had stood for years on top of the ramparts had caused considerable upset, nevertheless the inauguration of the new Park went a long way to making up for the loss:

> The above Park and Children's Recreation Ground was opened by the Mayor (W.D. King, Esq.) on April 25th, 1878. . .
> It is tastefully laid out, there is also (*sic*) two Drinking Fountains, Band Stand, and a Monument dedicated to Sir Charles Napier. Size of Park about 12 small acres . . .[4]

Victoria Park may well have been 'tastefully laid out', with the intention of attracting the children to the Recreation Ground it provided; more likely the young would have continued their games on street corners, as they had always done. They were in any case probably chased off, should their games become too riotous, as indeed were some other visitors to the Park. . .

The trouble came to light when the Parks and Open Spaces Committee was asked to provide free seats in the Park, to which the Committee replied that such seats were 'not an unmixed blessing, for it was not always the most choice people who sat in them'.

This discussion led on to the problem of music in the Park, played by the Town Band, which the Entertainments Committee recommended should give performances on Mondays, Wednesdays and Fridays. However:

> . . . should dancing take place the band should be immediately

withdrawn . . . Mr. Merritt said that there was a slight attempt at dancing at a recent concert, and that was immediately stopped. There were several games played, too, but the police stopped them, saying they were an infringement of the bye-laws.[5]

This might seem a rather harsh interpretation of the law, but under the heading, 'Romps in the Park', the report goes on to criticise the behaviour of those who attended the Town Band concert on the Monday evening, warning that if such behaviour continued the concerts would stop:

> The Park bye-laws prohibit games such as "kiss-in-the-ring" and "leap-frog", yet a certain number of the audience, despite warning, persisted in these amusements ...(and) there was a very considerable amount of dancing of a sort.

Such goings on were repeated on the Wednesday, and 'in consequence of the dangerous tendency of the rowdyism', the Mayor took advice from the Chief Constable and the Chairman of the Band and decided that, apart from a Sunday afternoon concert, the performances must be stopped.

A vocalist had been persuaded to take part in the concerts, in the hope that this would 'be the means of drawing a better class of people in the Park . . . but in spite of the excellent vocal renderings of Mr. Collings Bailey', dancing, singing and shouting began the moment the Band struck up.

Small wonder that the concerts were abandoned. However, some four weeks later the subject of music in the Park was brought up again and after much disucsssion it was agreed that:

> . . . the vexed question had now been satisfactorily settled – providing the patrons of the music adhere to the stipulations of the Committee . . . With a view to provide what they consider a public want, they decided that the Town Band should resume its evening concerts, but they will play upon the distinct understanding that there shall be absolutely no dancing. Directly dancing is indulged in the music will be stopped, and there will be no continuance of it in the future. The people therefore have the matter in their own hands . . . if there is any suggestion of dancing they will be deprived of the enjoyment.

Sounding like nothing so much as a displeased parent, the Committee brought to an end the saga of 'Music in the Park' with the announcement that 'The Band will play on Mondays, Wednesdays and Fridays'.

While their elders were dancing, or more properly listening to the Band, the children would be making their own amusement. The hoop was probably the most popular of toys, those for the boys made of iron, the girls of wood; there were tops, whipped into motion, or peg-tops with a cord wound round the neck, there were 'five stones' and marbles, streaked with colour and even more valuable than a long-life conker, and there was 'diabolo', two sticks joined by a cord on which rolled a kind of top to be spun high into the air.

Some boys played a form of football, they swam and fished, and they 'mudlarked' from the Hard. If there was a fight, they took off for Hamburg Square, a secluded spot off Daniel Street, where they could settle a dispute without fear of interruption; but for the real street urchin, the best game – 'Gingerbread' – was to be had by tying two front door knockers together, ringing the bell, and running away. . .

There were always spoil-sports hoping to put a stop to such high spirits, and one gentleman, the much-respected Rev. H. Lindsay Young, protested most vigorously at a sight he had witnessed in Prince George Street, '. . . numerous little girls dancing and kicking up their legs round a barrel organ'. He blamed such shameless behaviour on the 'awful effects of theatres on the Christian population of the town', and it is hardly surprising that some caustic response was forthcoming. A letter to the *Hampshire Telegraph*, signed 'Snodgrass', informed readers that:

> I have seen things nearly as bad myself in Portsmouth, but I have been afraid to write and tell you of them, as yours is a respectable family paper. But I saw a sight last Wednesday three weeks that froze the marrow of my bones – I believe that is the proper expression. A tiny lad of six was playing a wicked, common, tin whistle-pipe, while a girl of five hummed the air and the air, moreover was – but enough, for a grown man passing at the time actually patted (God forgive him) the female monster on the head! You could have knocked me down, Sir, with a telegraph pole, but none of these being to hand, I fell into the arms of a policeman.[6]

CONVERSATIONS ON A
WEDNESDAY AFTERNOON

I – 'Lily'

She was born in Essex, she says.

– Then when I grew up I was in domestic service, in Ilford, and Walthamstow, all sorts of places round London - till I got married; then we came down from Essex in 1918. I was nineteen in the January and we were married in the August. We had two years with the in-laws at Stamshaw, and then we moved to Portsea, to furnished rooms – all over the place we were - Hanover Street, Union Street, College Street . . .

– You lived in all those places?

– Yes. And Butcher Street and Kent Street. My husband'd never pay the rent, that's why. We were in furnished rooms; we had to pay 6s. 6d. a week in 1918 – only my husband never would pay, so we were always having to move on.

– Was he a Portsmouth man?

– Yes – he was invalided out of the Army, and after that he was a slaughterman. He used to bring home pigs' heads, and trotters, and chitterlings. They were full of worms, those chitterlings! You'd put them in salt water overnight and change the water next day; then you'd turn them inside out and boil them. I used to go round the houses selling those chitterlings at 1s. 6d. a plate.

– How did you do your cooking?

– Gas. And there was only gas lighting of course – no electricity. There was no bathroom either, and there was only the outside privy – well, all the toilets were outside in those days, weren't they? Outside in the yard.

– Tell me about your family. Did you have any children?

– One. My daughter. She was five months when we came to Portsea. She went to school at the 'Benny' first; then to the Kent Street School.

– That was a mixed school, wasn't it?

– No, it wasn't mixed! They used to keep the boys up one end and the girls the other. . . They'd give her dinners at the school, and at the Salvation Army they'd hand out the 'Farthing Breakfasts' for all the poor children - in Queen Street, that was . . . She and her husband, they had ten children. But then she died at forty-seven.

– Were you here in Portsea during the war?

– My husband had gone off with some woman by then . . . so after a while I took up with another man – . Why not?

– Why not!

– I was thirty-seven, and he was forty-two; we were together till he died at seventy-one. For a long time he'd been a slaughterman too, then later he worked as a fisherman.

– And what about the last war? Were you here through it all?

– Me and my daughter were evacuated to Surrey; we moved about quite a bit, from one billet to another. We were away four years altogether.

– Just the two of you?

– We were always together, me and my daughter – till she got married.

– What about your gentleman friend?

– During the war? He stayed on in Portsea, fire-fighting. He had four children, and I took on all four of them - a girl of nineteen (she was living away most of the time), one of sixteen, one of twelve, one of ten and one of five. They lived in the High Street, and I remember the tide used to come in, right up to the door, and the children would be taken by boat and rowed down the High Street to the school; that school was somewhere where the Power Station used to be.

– Can you remember anything about Christmas? Did you have turkey on Christmas Day?

– No, we didn't have turkey – we'd have duck sometimes, or maybe a goose. We used to go up to the market, and take a sack for oranges and nuts and dates and figs. Oranges were twenty for a shilling. But we didn't have turkey. . .

II – 'Hilda'

– Yes, I was born here, in Portsea. I was Hilda Perrin before I was married. We lived in Hawke Street before the first World War. My Dad ran a pub on the Hard; I can't remember the name of it - it was shut down years ago. After he was a publican, my Dad was a bookie.

– Tell me something about your family.

– My grandfather – his name was Farlow; he was a greengrocer in Queen Street. I had two brothers – one died at birth, the other, Jimmy, he died at twenty-one in an accident; he was knocked down by a Brickwood's lorry. Then I had a step-sister, and she died in Malta.

– What do you remember about your home when you were a girl?

What was it like in Hawke Street?

– Same as now – different people, of course, but much the same. We cooked by gas, I remember, and we had gas lighting as well, till they put us on the electric.

– Was there a bathroom in the house?

– No. There was a bath downstairs, and we kept it covered over all day, and just took the cover off when we wanted a bath. And the toilet was outside of course; we had a small garden out at the back and the toilet was out there.

– Some of the houses used to have their kitchen in the basement. That must have been awful – .

– No, we didn't have a basement at our place.

– Tell me about your school days.

– First I went to Mrs. Logan's in Union Street; that was a private school, and you had to pay 6d. a week to go there. She taught the piano, and she used to try and teach us our lessons at the same time; there weren't many of us, and we didn't learn very much! Then I went to the Circus School. Years ago when the circus came to town their children were sent there. It's where Pinks is now. . .

– Tell me about your mother. Did she go out to work?

– No. . . I remember one thing about my Mum – she liked Gorgonzola cheese, and one day as I was going off to school she said, 'Get me some of the Gorgonzola cheese, will you?' so I went and bought it and took it to school with me; the teacher complained of the smell and she kept walking round the room, till she came to me and she sniffed and said, 'Have you messed yourself?' and I said 'No!', but I didn't ever tell her about the cheese.

– What did you do at school, beside ordinary lessons? Did you have singing, or drawing, or needlework?

– We did needlework, on a Monday afternoon; we called it 'Garments'.

– What sort of garments?

– Just 'garments' – nightdresses and that. And all done by hand. We didn't use sewing machines. And I used to go to Cookery lessons in Arundel Street, one penny a week it was. On Pancake Day we were told how to toss the pancakes, and I tossed mine and it went up in the air and landed on the gas bracket, and it was all dripping down! The teacher wasn't a bit amused, but we all were.

During the war (the first war) we had a foreign lady to teach us – Austrian, I think she was – and she taught us how to scrub the wooden kitchen tables, and she'd run her hand over it to make sure it was really clean; I thought it was funny having a foreign lady, in wartime.

– Did you have school dinners?

– There was no such thing in those days. We'd go home for our dinners.

– What happened after you left school?

– I'd left school at fourteen. Later, in the war, I went to Coventry, to the Coventry Ordnance Depot on munitions. First thing I saw as I came out of the station was a big statue of Lady Godiva; it was beautiful, but I thought, 'Oh, fancy, a thing like that outside the station!' I remember the zeppelin coming over, and we were all afraid it'd drop a bomb on the explosives and blow us all up - and all Coventry as well.

– What else do you remember about your mother?

– She was one of seven daughters. Her father had a pub in Old Portsmouth.

– Did she like to do a lot of baking at home?

– No, not a lot. But she was very sorry for the people in the alley behind us, and if one of them was sick she used to send round food to them – brawn and that sort of thing. We always had plenty.

– What about Christmas? Did you have a good time at Christmas?

– I remember one Christmas during the war we were disgusted! Mum had left the turkey till the last minute, and when we got to the butcher (we had the same butcher as is there now) he said, 'There's nothing left except this bit of brisket!' and I was given a bit of brisket of lamb!

– For Christmas Day?

– That's all he had left. And so we had brisket that Christmas. . . I remember Dad often liked to have a bit of rabbit pie, put on a plate at his side. He bred his own rabbits, and I had a favourite rabbit; I used to call everything that came into the house 'Jimma', and my rabbit was called 'Jimma'. One day Dad was eating his pie and he said, 'Jimma tastes good!' and I said, 'This isn't Jimma, is it?' and he said, 'Yes!'. I couldn't eat any more, and I cried and cried.

– What pocket money did you get?

– I didn't *get* it – I had to ask for it! When I was sixteen or seventeen, I'd ask my Dad for money: 'Give me a shilling,' I'd say, and we'd go to Clarence Pier, mostly, on a Sunday night. It was called the 'Monkey's Parade', Sunday night at Clarence Pier. Sometimes on a Sunday we'd go to see the Fusiliers on parade in Old Portsmouth; it was a hive of activity down there, with all the girls in their new frocks. . . ! As we went down the High Street, we used to see an old Chinaman sitting in his window, and we used to make faces at him and run away. Unkind, it was really, but we used to do it.

– Did you often go on holiday?

– No. we didn't often go away from Portsmouth. I went to Shanklin Chine once. It was lovely there. The second time I went, I was with a fellow I was engaged to. He'd gone to work there, and he was in lodgings. Well, as we were driving up a hill, something went wrong with the car; he got out and climbed underneath, and the brakes went and the car ran over him.

– You were there when this happened?

– Yes, I was there . . . I went over once more, to his funeral. But no more. I didn't go to the Island again.

– But then, eventually, you did get married? Tell me about your wedding day.

– We got married at St. George's Church. I went to Sunday School there when I was younger. It was a big wedding. . .

– Did you wear white?

– Oh yes, and we had the reception at Long's Memorial Hall in St. Paul's Square. My husband had come ashore, and we had the Marines Band, and they tied sixteen old sea boots behind the car! And when we went off on our honeymoon, my Dad put a £5 note on the table to spend on my honeymoon.

– Where did you live afterwards?

– I had a flat above the Camden Hotel. One time we lived at Bonfire Corner, but I was married from Havant Street; a big old-fashioned house it was on four floors. I remember a big fire at Camper and Nicholson, and we could see all the flames from the top floor of our house. . . I remember when I was in my teens, there was that 'Spanish 'flu' period, and we had a young boy of eighteen staying in the house at the time. He was ill in bed up there on the top floor, and Mum said to me, 'He's been shouting and bawling all night! I didn't know what to do with him.' His bed was sort of in a cupboard, and he kept looking up and saying 'This b— train is slow!', and trying to get out of bed; so I told him to get back in and stay there, and so he would for a bit . . .

There was another young fellow taken ill; we didn't know who he was because his mate, who lived with us, had brought him to the house. Anyway, he died, and we didn't know what to do; but they found his mother, and she came and accused us of robbing him. 'Where's his watch and chain?' she kept saying, and we told her, he'd not had it while he was with us. She was going all on for a long time, and I don't think she ever believed us. . .

– You were saying about when you got married.

– I was twenty-one when I got married. My husband was in the Royal Marines Band. I liked the Band! When I was at school, you could hear the Band in the Barracks as they took down the Ensign, and I used to run all the way from school, just to hear the Band play. . .

– Did you have any children?

– I had three – Tony was the eldest, then Sheila. I'd never heard that name before till one night when I was expecting we went to the Arcade, to the pictures. It was the last night of my husband's leave, and there was a photograph on the wall of a film star called Sheila something, and I said, 'If I have a girl, I'm going to call her Sheila'. She was born at the Royal Naval Maternity Home; and then there was Brian, or 'Bill' as we call him. He was born at St. Mary's, and when he arrived someone said 'Who's making all that noise?' and they were told it was the new baby, and they said, 'What, a baby with a voice like that?' He weighed thirteen pounds and they said he should be called Battling Bill' – because he was so big and he was born with his fists clenched, like *that* !

– What about the last war?

– We made an air raid shelter in the garden, to our own design. But Mum would never go down it; she used to say, 'If you've got to go, you've got to go!' I was in the WRNS in the last war, as a cook; I was living in London at the time, and we were told that all the children were to be evacuated; two of mine were sent to Northampton, my Tony and 'Battling Bill', and I remember we mothers were made to stop at the barrier while the children got on the train. I was crying my eyes out, and I can still see Billy turning to look back at me, saying 'What's up with my Mummy? What's she crying for?' . . .

You won't believe this – I used to play football, with Portsmouth Ladies! Ada Anscombe got up a team during the war; she had seven brothers and so she knew about football. We used to train quite hard, and once we played the 10th London Regiment – all professionals they were. We played on Portsdown Hill, in a farmer's field which was on a slope, so if you gave the ball a 'header' it used to roll for miles! Sometimes we went to the Portsdown Fair; Hesketh's, where the paper shop is in Queen Street, they used to let bikes out for 1s. an hour, and we'd go up to Portsdown that way. There used to be lots of shops in Queen Street, in those days . . .

III – 'Charlie'

I worked at Brickwoods. I started at fourteen in the mineral water factory in Daniel Street, and one of my jobs was on the horse and cart – I'd have to sit outside the public house with a ginger beer and crisps while the delivery was going on and sometimes the driver came out drunk, and he'd climb up on the cart, and he'd just flick the reins and the horse would bring us back to Hamburg Square, all on his own. That was Fred Clay, the driver.

When I was eighteen they transferred me to the brewery; the manager was a man called Evans - he said there were no vacancies for me, because it was a family firm then, and jobs were kept for people to do with the family. But then Evans said, hadn't I got a brother and a sister working upstairs, and a mother who'd worked there in the 1914-18 war? And I said, yes, and he said, 'Why not say so, then!' and I got a job in the painters' shop.

Sometimes they used to call you out to go on the transport if one of the regulars hadn't turned up. We'd go out on the Foden – the driver was a man called Cox, the mate was Fred Clay, who'd got himself transferred to the brewery, and I was the 'boy'.

That big Foden was steam driven - the first three-wheeler in the town. They also had a four-wheeler and a six-wheeler, and later they went over to Austin. The Foden just had lettering on the side at first, then they invented the Sunshine Ale, so they used the 'Sunshine' logo; that started about 1926 or so.

We'd clock in at 6.30 in the morning, and after we'd loaded up Cox would light up the fire, and then we'd go and have a cup of tea in the café on the corner of Prince George's Street. Then we'd come back and trundle over to Southampton; we'd leave at 8.0 and go on our way – at six miles per hour! We'd have to stop half way for water, and then we'd get there about midday. We had to deliver to three public houses, and then we'd come home again, getting back about 6.0.

After we'd unloaded the lorry, it was my job to wash the wheels, and all over the body; we got the water from the scalding yard – Fred Clay would break up the wood from old boxes, to light the fire next morning, and we'd finish about seven in the evening. Then at 6.30 the next morning, we'd start all over. We got overtime, of course, if we were late back. When I was eighteen, in about 1930-31, I got paid 12s. 6d. a week, the mate about 18s. and the driver, 25s..

I retired after forty-two years service, including war-time in the R.A.F., and afterwards I did some bar cellar work at the Esplanade near South Parade Pier, and at the Albany in Commercial Road. Then Whitbreads offered me this place where I live now in St. George's Square; it used to be a public house, the *Eagle*, till they turned it into flats. My sitting room was the bar!

How did we boys spend our free time? That'd be around 1925 – we used to go to the 'Bullring', by Clarence Pier; they called it that, because the dance band was in the middle and you'd dance in a circle all around. We'd stand in the entrance, four or five of us, and wait till we could see an unattached girl dancing with someone; then if she was a good dancer one of us'd ask her to dance.

Then sometimes we'd go to the cinema - there was the Queen's in Queen Street, I remember, and the manager was a man called Lewis; one chap would take the money to go in, and he'd get a ticket and go down by the screen to the fire exit, then he'd open the door and let the rest of us in for nothing!

I played football and cricket for Brickwoods, and for the Rotary Club. And I was *News of the World* darts champion for this area, and Hampshire runner up, and after the war I was Brickwoods champion three years running! We used to play at the Rotary, at their club in Albert Street, and when that was bought by Brickwoods they moved to Butcher Street, next to the *Eagle*.

I remember the Salvation Army took over the *Royal Oak Tree* pub in Unicorn street, and they'd serve the Farthing Breakfasts from there, before you went to school. But we didn't have those because my father had been a C.P.O. Bos'un in the Navy, and Farthing Breakfasts were only for the hard-up families - same thing with the Boot Club. My father had a Navy pension, after twenty-two years service, and then he went to work in the Dockyard so we were what you might call 'middle class'; I remember once some boys thought I was wearing Boot Fund boots, and they didn't think that was right, with my father working; but I told them they weren't Boot Fund boots, my father'd bought them – so then we got down to fisticuffs! But I won –!

My father was very strict, being in the Navy, and he'd never let us go mudlarking. But I remember once, when I was very small, I nearly got drowned, playing on the wooden bridge that used to run under the railway station down by the Hard; there was a chap talking to my brother while he was casting his fishing line, and one of these lines was lying on the ground, so I picked it up threw it in the water. I knew I'd done wrong, and I was so scared I just walked straight into the water after it! I was only three at the time, but I can remember it clearly – it must have been the fright that makes me remember it. Anyway, Mick, my brother, hauled me out - my mother was working in the cellar at the brewery and someone said to her, 'Little Charlie had a lucky escape', and that was the first she heard of it. She gave me a good hiding!

She was half French, my mother; her name was Le Cointe, and her mother was German – worked for Queen Victoria at Osborn House for a time. My grandfather was a Master Armourer at 'Vernon' and he met my grandmother in India; she could make very good curries! When he retired he took a bicycle shop in Southsea, hiring out bikes.

There were four of us - my brother and me and two sisters; one sister married a C.P.O. in the Royal Yacht, the *Victoria and Albert*, that is. If your father was in the Navy, he'd be away at sea two-and-a-half years – that's probably why there's seven years between us children!

I had diptheria, scarlet fever - you name it, I had it. I used to have lovely long auburn curls down to my shoulders as a baby, but they had some idea that when you got diptheria part of the cure was to cut off all your hair; and when I left the hospital, we were coming home in a landau, and my cousin saw me, but she didn't recognise me without my curls!

We lived at No.25 Unicorn Street; we were tenants there, but we had to move when they demolished the houses, and they found tunnels to the Dockyard underneath them, for all the smuggling that went on in the Unicorn Gate area.

Yes, I remember the murders! Police didn't take much notice if a prostitute got murdered; I remember there was one at the *Bedford* pub, on the corner of Church Path. A sailor came ashore unexpected and found the prostitute with another sailor, so he pulled out a razor and cut her throat.

The first one I remember was when I was coming home from school – I'd started school at Kent Street, but I used to get caned there a lot, so later I went to St. John's – I was coming down North Street when I saw a policeman with two bloodhounds. The prostitute who'd been

'… on the pavement by the Hard…'
(Portsmouth Polytechnic Central Photography Unit)

Launch of the Iron Duke, October 1912, Greasers on the 'Grease' Track.
(Portsmouth Polytechnic Central Photography Unit)

murdered was called 'Bath Alice', because she'd come from Bath in the first place. There were prostitutes in all those alleys - Blossom Alley, Chatham Row, York Place - there were one or two in every street, two in Unicorn Street, one called Rose and the other was a French girl called Marie. 'Jack' would get paid once a fortnight, but on a blank week, the prostitutes would often feel sorry for them and buy them a pint to tide them over. They were very good to the sailors, some of those girls.

IV – 'Mrs. Clarke'

My father didn't take over the *Ship Anson* till I was about ten; before that we'd lived in a big house in Milford Road, with a tailor's workshop at the back. There were twenty-three people in that workshop! My father was a tailor - he worked for Gieves and Hawkes, making gold braid for the cadets' uniforms; but then he decided to take the *Ship Anson down* on the Hard.

He used to open the pub at six o'clock in the morning, for the men going to work in the Dockyard; but he still kept a workroom at the top of the house, to keep his tailoring going. I don't remember too much about the pub because my father died two years after we got there.

He'd always been a rather strict man; there was 'no talking at the table', and I remember a picture of Noah's Ark over the mantlepiece, with a cane tucked into it – and if we were naughty at table, he'd just have to point at the cane and that'd make us behave! But he never actually had to use it on us.

When my sister Winnie was a baby I used to mind her sometimes; I'd take her to sit on the pavement by the Hard while I played on the bit of beach – she'd have her legs dangling over, and it's a wonder she never fell in the water! The boatman there was a Mr. Daniels, and he'd take visitors out midstream to the *Victory* for sixpence a time; if the boat wasn't full he'd take some of the local children with him sometimes. In those days, before the first World War, you could get to the Isle of Wight for 1s. 6d. by paddle steamer, and the Gosport Ferry would cost you one ha'penny.

My mother had a bad time of it in the early days, because there were six of us children in the family; I was the eldest at twelve and the youngest was fourteen months when my father died. Some time before, a Mr. Martin had come to my father to have his suits made, and because he was in insurance, he persuaded my father to place his insurance with him – but Father died only twelve months later and this meant my mother wasn't entitled to claim. The solicitor said my mother should sue, which she did, but she not only lost, she had to pay the costs for both sides. So then there was no money, and she had to sell the house to settle the debt.

Dolly Beaver was a girl who used to come in and work for my mother, looking after us children; she was only fourteen, a tiny thing, and she had several brothers and sisters of her own, so she'd go home to help her mother after work, then return to us at 9.00. in the evening.

After we left the *Ship Anson* we went to live in King Street for a few weeks, then we moved to Hanover Street; most of Portsea was very much a slum area at that time, before the first war, but Hanover Street was considered a good area, like Union Street, where the houses were mostly occupied by professional people. But my mother had no pension, so she had to take in boarders; two of them, I remember, were a Mr. Smith and a Mr. Cocking.

I went to the Free School off Lion Terrace. We did as we were told in those days! And if we were naughty, we had to stand up straight in front of the class with our hands behind our backs. We had dinner at school, bread and cheese on Wednesdays and soup on Friday; it was free, but we never looked on it as charity! People used to come round collecting for the Boot Fund, for the poor children who had to go barefoot – and that was quite a common thing in those days.

We used to do a play at Christmas; and we had cookery classes, and needlework classes two afternoons a week; you were never given a reel of thread to work with – but if you were a monitor you'd stand out in front with your apron on and you'd have a reel of coloured thread in one pocket and a reel of white in the other, and when someone needed some more thread, you just break off a piece and hand it to them!

We didn't go to the cinema or anything like that – it was too expensive. But there was a passage-way leading off Hanover Street, with several big houses standing empty, and that's where the children used to play most of the time. And of course there were the mudlarks down in the harbour; when the tide was low they used to beg from the people walking down the pontoon, calling to them 'Throw a penny in the mud, sir!' and then they'd dive in and retrieve the coins from the mud.

I used to go to the Portsdown Fair with my friend, Katherine Neate, and sometimes the boys would treat us to a ride on the merry-go-round. We had to walk all the way there and all the way back! But we never told our mothers where we were going - and they didn't ask because they thought we'd gone to stay in each other's house!

I remember Dad sold antiques and pictures from time to time; there was one picture in the front room, and after he'd gone, a man came to ask my mother if she'd sell it, and she let him have it for five pounds. It wasn't till later we were told it was a Constable . . .

V – 'Jock'

– I was born in Stamshaw. A 'Stamshaw Chicken' – that's what I am – but if you don't know what that is, I can't tell you! It's a bit rude . . .

– Tell me about where you lived, then.

– We went up to Edinburgh during the first war, but then we came back in 1926 and we went to live in St. George's Square first , in rooms; then we went to Hawke Street for a bit, then back to St. George's Square, in a flat. It was a big flat, too – ran right on through, from the front to the back; and it was curtained off into five or six rooms. There was just me and my parents at that time, so there was plenty of room.

– What did your father do?

– He was a shipwright in the Dockyard. Sometimes, when there wasn't any work, he'd have to go over to Southampton every day, to the Docks there to look for work, with the big liners coming in. He'd go by train, of course. It'd cost him , workman's ticket, 1s. 0½d; and he'd only be getting about 25s. a week at the time . . . And then he had to leave work at sixty, and he hadn't got in enough time for a pension.

– How did you manage?

– We always fed well enough. Meat was cheap, and the old man grew vegetables on the allotment out at Hilsea. He'd take the pram and I'd go on the bike and sometimes we'd come back with two, three hundred-weight of potatoes. I remember once when we were coming back there was a raid on; they hit the Prince's Cinema in Lake Road – it was lucky we weren't there at the time.

– Tell me more about the food.

– You could get a loaf for 2½d. Jimmy Yates was the owner of Campion's Bakery, and after the roundsmen got back you could go round to the shop and the bread would all be sorted out and you'd be given a loaf for 2½d or even 2d. And you could go to the vegetable shop for a pennyworth of mixed herbs, onion, carrot, turnip – or we'd catch a bit of fish, from the boat. I've had a boat, since I was a young man, a 14ft. boat.

– Where did you fish from?

– Mostly in the harbour. But if you wanted skate, you had to go outside for that. . . The shellfishermen used to take their catch up to Charlotte Street, and some of us'd go 'long-lining' for whelks. You'd spend a day on the mud collecting small crabs, and thread them on a string, then take the boat out into the Solent and throw the line over-board. Nowadays you get whelk pots – they put any old bit of fish in and the whelks get themselves into the pot to feed. But we used long lengths of line.

– You mentioned the wherrymen – .

– The wherrymen would take visitors round the harbour, or to see the *Victory* when she was still in the water; there was Ernie Daniels – he lived in Havant Street, so did Jack Bamber, and there was Harry Mears, he lived in College Street. There was a rest house for the cabbies and the wherrymen on the Hard, on the wooden bridge to the railway station. Then there were the bumboat men – when a ship came in, decommissioned, they'd row out to Spithead to meet her. They'd take fish and chips out to the sailors, and if the ship arrived on a Sunday, they'd take out the Sunday papers. When a ship was being launched, there were always boatmen waiting down by the slipway to collect the tallow and bits of timber.

– What did they do with the tallow?

– They'd sell it to the rag merchants, and the timber went to the coal merchant . . . Then there were the Navy pinnaces, 'double enders' they were called, and three quarters of them had real brass funnels. There's still one in the Dockyard now.

– Tell me about your first job.

– I pushed a barrow for a wholesale grocer - King's on the Hard. I used to get about 6s. a week, there; I was offered 5s. as an apprentice to an awning-maker, Littlefield's in Fratton Road, but King's were paying more! And every penny counted in those days. That's where I lost my right eye, at King's, chopping firewood. My mother put a tea-leaf poultice on it to draw it, but it didn't work, so the doctor sent me to the Eye and Ear Hospital in Pembroke Road. I was off work for a long time after that, but I didn't go back to King's; I was labouring till I went to the Dockyard – I helped with the foundations for the G.P.O. in Chichester.

– What did you do in the Dockyard?

– 'Slinging'. That's putting the heavy machinery back into place in the boats. They'd take the main engines out of the boats or the submarines or whatever ship it was, and when they were ready to go back, then the big crane would lift the engine, and we'd see it got back into place. This would be about 1939. I remember I was a 'slinger' on the *Queen Elizabeth* when she was in the Dockyard for a refit in the early part of the war. I was up and down that mast like a monkey! Every time the sirens went I had to shin down, and then as soon as we heard the all clear, it was back up again. . . We took her up to Rosyth at Christmas in 1940, then to the Flow where she had her trials . . .

– What happened if you had an accident? Or if you got ill? Did you have any insurance?

– We paid threepence a week 'Hospital' money. Then if you were sick and needed an appointment, you'd go to the Collector and ask for a letter, then you'd take the letter to the hospital, and that would show you were paid up.

– Who was the Collector?

– Just someone the men appointed. The old fellow we had came from Portchester.

– When you first came back from Edinburgh, which school did you go to?

– The 'Benny'. There was one big room, one on each floor, divided by partitions, and there was one teacher to each group. Later they used to have 'monitors' to help, but not in my day.

– Did you wear uniform?

Steam Launches in Portsmouth Harbour.
(Portsmouth Polytechnic Central Photography Unit)

The Vicar and Choir, St. George's Church, c.1926.
(Property of Mr. 'Jock' Hoare)

– Not in those days! Couldn't afford it.

– Did you have school dinners?

– Some of the 'Benny' boys got free dinners. And free boots – you could get one pair of boots a year if you were really hard up. Yes, there used to be quite a bit of feeling against the boys who got free meals and free boots – animosity, mostly! We'd say, why should he get boots and we didn't? And some of the children could go to the Salvation Army for the 'Farthing Breakfast'. That was in Daniel Street They were very good if you were in trouble; I remember there was a lady who lived with my mother; she went into hospital and when she came back she was *'potless'!*

– Potless?

– No money. She went to the Salvation Army and they took her in at a place in Auckland Road – very clean and polished, it was. I was sent there once, as an errand boy, so I saw for myself . . . . My mother's first husband was a navvy, often out of work, and he'd just paid the first week of his Benefit when he got sick; the Salvation Army came to my mother and asked her to join, and she said she couldn't afford to, so the Salvation Army paid the first instalment of benefit.. They did a lot of good for people.

– What games did you play at school?

– In the yard, kicking a football around.

– Did you play games like Hopscotch?

– No, we didn't play hopscotch! It was a boy's school! But we did play cricket. Mr. Thomas was famous for his cricket.

– That's him, in the St. George's photograph, near the back?

– Yes. He used to give us batting practise in break time and dinner time. 'Daniel' Thomas was a schoolmaster at the 'Benny'; there's Len Knight and Jim Quick to the left of the Vicar, and Bob Clieff and Bill May down at the front - and 'Ear Whacker'! His real name was Earwicker, but we called him 'Ear Whacker' . . .that's Cyril May in front of the Vicar, and Harry Fulthorpe's at the end of the row - he did a Dockyard apprenticeship and sea time in the Navy, then he came back to be Manager of the Dockyard . . .

– Did you play cricket against other schools?

– We had a school team, and we'd play matches on the Common. Or we'd play amongst ourselves, in the street. We used to play 'Tip It' on St. George's Square; you'd have two sticks, one long and one short, abvout five inches and tapered at the end; someone'd throw the short one to you and you'd have to hit it and when it landed in the ground you'd go out and tap it on the end, and when it came up you'd hit it again. You'd do this three times and if the other fellow could get it back to 'home' in three strides, you were out.

– A bit like Rounders – .

– No, not a bit like Rounders!

– Did you often go to the Cinema?

– Sometimes. That'd cost 1d. or 2d. We didn't like the Victoria Hall Cinema – you'd get lousy! Sometimes we might go to the variety at the Coliseum in Edinburgh Road - the 'fourpenny touch' we called that. And we'd go fishing off the pontoon; I remember Solly Joel coming over from the Island, walking along that pontoon. You know Solly Joel? He went in for horse racing; he'd come down for Goodwood in July, and I believe he had a yacht over on the Island. Used to go over there for Cowes week. . . Solly'd come to the steps at the side of the pontoon, and one of the 'scruffs' would be waiting for him; he was a hard case, that one – nobody dared go near him – and he'd hold open the door of Solly Joel's Rolls for him as he came off the boat . . . And we'd sometimes see Tommy Sopwith; his boat was built at Camper and Nicholson – my father worked on his boats.

– Do you remember the Schneider Tropy?

– Yes! Being a Rotary boy, the caretaker of the club let us up on the roof to watch the first one. On another occasion, my sister was friendly with a sailor, and he'd come home, and he asked 'would we like a trip out on his boat to see Trophy Day?' That was H.M.S. *Sabre*, a turtle-back destroyer. Me and a friend went out with them past Selsey, to the turning point, and we could see them coming down and all the way back again! And we were on duty-free cigarettes too!

– What about school outings?

– We didn't have many of those. We went to the Waterworks at Bedhampton once. And then, of course, I went to Rotary Camp. Rotary Boys were a pack that the Inner Wheel looked after – they were gentlemen in those days, in the Inner Wheel; there was a Club in Butcher Street, with boxing and snooker. Frank Leak looked after the boxing, he was the trainer. Upstairs there was snooker, and above that, ping-pong. Every Friday night Jimmy Yates of Campions came and played Shove Ha'penny with some of the boys, and you always got a cup of tea and a sticky bun from him afterwards. He was a gentleman, and so was Mr. Martin; he had a wholesale warehouse - haberdashery, and materials – in Stanhope Road. And then there was Mr. Evans, wholesale washing powders and soap and bleaches; he was in York Street till after the war then he went to Fratton Road. Later, I saw his vans and lorries came from Worthing, or Brighton – somewhere along there. There were lots like them, helping at the Club.

– Tell me about Rotary Camp.

– We went to annual camp for a week at Hayling Island; they had a site at the end of Fishery Lane, with a barn where the food was served for you. We slept in tents, but in bad weather we all went into the barn. There was a keeper there with a gun on hand for ferrets and stoat; he had a pet rabbit, I remember. And there was a man with the Rotary called 'Lobby Ludd', a South African; he'd come to camp in his car, and he'd fetch and carry in that car, and run someone back home if they needed something, and he'd take the whole team in the car sometimes!

– What else do you remember?

– I remember when we were boys, sixteen, seventeen, we'd get up at four o'clock on Sunday mornings and make ice cream for old Valerio, at his shop in Butcher Street; we'd mix up the milk, eggs, cornflour, sometimes a bit of vanilla root and the old man would take it in a barrow to Church Path. During the week my mate'd do all the steaming of the milk if the old boy was not feeling well; he'd boil the milk, add the eggs and the cornflour, and when it was cooked he'd put it out in an enamel pail and leave it in the cooler till it was wanted. There weren't any fridges in those days! The cooler was one of those wooden meat safes with a gauze front. It was hanging up on the wall, and he'd put the ice cream in there to cool off. It would last a couple of nights, maybe. . .

– What else?

– I was going to tell you about the washerwomen – they used to take a pram to the Dockyard, and they'd be allowed in so they could go on board. None of the ships had laundries, so the women used to collect the washing in the evening and and take it back home with them. The ships had a round hole in the deck and the women would shout down the hole, 'Any dirties?', and the sailors'd give them their laundry, possibly with a bit of soap to wash with. And they'd have it back again next day, cleaned and ironed, whatever the weather! I'll never know how they managed it, in the bad weather.

– Where did they live, these women?

– Two or three lived in Havant Street, and Landport – they'd go in the Dockyard through the Unicorn Gate. They did all the washing in a copper; they'd go to the cardboard box makers and get off-cuts in a sack, to boil up the copper. There'd be an old mangle, and a scrub board, and those 'dolly' pegs, and they'd dry the things on an airer screwed into the ceiling that you could let down on a pulley . . . But I'll never know how they managed to get everything dry and ironed and back again next morning!

THE CLOUDS OF WAR

All those years of unemployment, of poor housing and little health care were gradually being replaced by all-round improvement that, given a clear run, would have meant vastly better circumstances for the people who lived and worked and died in the poorer parts of the City. But war came, twice in a lifetime, and priorities had to change.

In the First World War there was an acute shortage of labour in the City, and for the first time women stepped in to fill the gaps, acting as postwomen, van drivers and munitions workers, displaying what was referred to as a 'hitherto unsuspected aptitude for manly occupations'. They deputised for tram drivers and conductors, not in the least put off when the *Evening News* expressed concern for the uncomfortable and unattractive uniform they were obliged wear: 'The Corporation should be ashamed ... how these poor girls suffer' and went on to suggest that they be equipped with a more light-weight uniform.[1] Women were in the Police Force, there were even women working in the Dockyard; at the start of the war there had been only fifty in all, but by 1918 this figure had increased to more than 1700, including a select few working on the Block Mills.

But post-war all the old problems returned – inadequate housing, unemployment, a general dissatisfaction that was to continue until the mid-1930s, when once again the clouds of war came rolling in.

As early as 1935 the Government had begun to make plans against the possibility of war, recognising the need for a better fire service, for rescue services, and even for anti-gas squads. But if war came the first priority would be to get the children away from the City; in September 1938 a meeting was held to discuss 'Action re Children in the event of an air raid', and in the following July the Council set up a highly successful 'Evacuation Test'. At the time no one could have guessed that only a few weeks later evacuation would no longer be an exercise.

On 1 September 1939, Kent Street Boys' School was 'assembled for

'*Women Workers, Block Mills. Dockyard, Portsmouth*', *First World War.*
(*Portsmouth Royal Dockyard Historical Society*)

Evacuation of the children, 1939.
(*By courtesy of The News, Portsmouth*)

evacuation at 7.30 a.m.. Left Portsmouth Town Station, by bus, at 8.20. Destination – Basingstoke area'. One boy, a pupil at the School, described the day he left Portsea:

> We were taken by bus to Portsmouth town railway station and told by our master, Mr. Cooper, that we were going to Basingstoke. We were each issued with a tin of corned beef and a packet of biscuits, and threatened not to eat them in case we did not get accommodation...
>
> From Basingstoke, we were taken by bus to Silchester and seated in the village hall, where the parishoners came to select whom they would like to come and live with them.
>
> I can remember seeing my friends paired off with different families, and, eventually, a lady and gentleman and their two children approached me and asked if I could like to live with them.[2]

War was now a fact, but since it did not immediately affect the safety of ordinary people in the City, the children began to drift back home. Parents were warned of the danger and largely chose to ignore such warnings, so that when at last the raids began, they had to face the upset of evacuation all over again. As the Lord Mayor had said in a letter written back in October:

> The most fitting judgement on evacuation was that it was a well intentioned scheme, which, though a successful experience for a few, can generally be regarded as a failure.[3]

The first Official Notice, issued by the War Emergency Committee, appeared on 2 September 1939:

> 1. *Shelters* In these neighbourhoods, principally in the centre of the City and Portsea, where the erection of Anderson Shelters is difficult, and the gardens are too small for digging a trench, it is proposed to erect sand-bagged communal shelters in the street...

People were advised to 'Avoid asking questions', and to 'keep off the streets as much as possible':

> ... In the event of an air attack, take cover. If no public shelter is near at hand, any householder will let you have such protection as his house affords...[4]

On a summer's night in 1940, Portsea came under fire from enemy

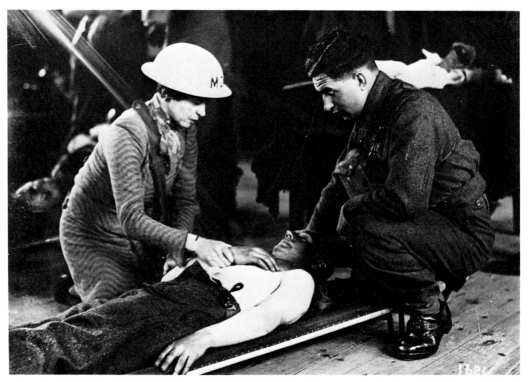

Dr. Una Mulvaney, medical officer in charge of a First Aid Post in St. George's Square, 'on duty in every raid (she) risked her life again and again. Bombs had no terror for this brave Portsmouth doctor, whom the King honoured with the M.B.E.'
(By courtesy of The News, 3 March 1980)

'They kept smiling down at Bonfire Corner'.
(By courtesy of The News, Portsmouth)

aircraft. In St. George's Square there was a direct hit on the public shelter, and it was something of a miracle that there was only one casualty, a boy of fifteen. At Bonfire Corner many of the people were driven from their homes:

> Bonfire Corner . . . was one of the first areas of Portsmouth hit by enemy raiders . . . People salvaged furniture and belongings from their homes after the second raid on Portsmouth, on August 12th.
>
> In 20 minutes, 25 bombers punished Portsea, Old Portsmouth, and parts of Southsea as well as Gosport and the Isle of Wight . . . The death toll in Portsmouth was 13, and 100 were injured; and the City realized what world War Two was likely to bring.
>
> But they kept smiling, down at Bonfire Corner'.[5]

This raid, and many others, was vividly captured in the diary[6] of a young, unfortunately anonymous schoolgirl who recorded faithfully many of the incidents taking place around the City:

> Aug. 12 We had an air raid at 9.20 a.m. & another at 12.0 noon. The second one was terrific. There was heavy gunfire and lots of bombs dropped. The harbour station was hit & St. Johns church in the dockyard was burnt to the ground. . . A bomb fell near H.M.S. Victory but did no damage. The place where Mrs. Batchelor works was blown in.

There is no clue to the whereabouts of 'the place where Mrs. Batchelor works', but the diarist's account of the damage is at once so extraordinary and yet so typical of many similar incidents, that it is worth reading on to the end of that day:

> Solid mahogany doors 5-6 ins thick were blown off there (*sic*) hinges to the other side of the room. The wardrobes were imbedded with glass from the windows. A tree was blown from the garden next door onto what WAS their roof. The back of the house was demolished completely. The lavatory pan was cut in half but the medicine bottles and shaving stick were left standing. In one cupboard there was pounds & pounds of marmalade, but all that happened was that the jars had moved forward about 4 ins. . .
>
> Also 7 lb pots of jam were blown from the table on to the floor right way up & never even broke. Mrs. Batchelor was nearly killed when the trap door to the cellar blew out and all the tiles from the fireplace came down in front of her. . . There were lots of fires started.

By the end of 1940 the daytime air raids had been abandoned because of bad weather: but though Portsea Island had already endured more than its fair share of air raids, and although 'they kept smiling, down at Bonfire Corner' – for the people living there the war had only just begun . . .

Bibliography
Unless otherwise stated, all books listed
were published in Portsmouth

Barfoot, T. 'Portsmouth and the Great War', typescript study, n.d..

Barnett, G.E. and Blanchard, V. *City of Portsmouth Records of the Corporation, 1936-45* (Corporation of Portsmouth).

Besant, W. and Rice, J. *By Celia's Arbour: A Tale of Portsmouth Town*, (London, Sampson Low, Searle & Rivington, 1878).

Carpenter, K.F. 'Public Health in Portsmouth, 1873-1900', unpublished dissertation, Faculty of Education Studies, Portsmouth Polytechnic, 1979.

Cramer, J. 'Messrs. Treadgold of Portsea Town', dissertation for Portsmouth Polytechnic Diploma in English Local History, 1982.

Department of Employment *British Labour Statistics*, (London, HMSO, 1971).

Digby, A. *Poor Law in Nineteenth Century England and Wales*, (London, 1982).

Dolling, R.R. *Ten Years in a Portsmouth Slum*, (6th edition, London, Brown, Langham, 1903).

Durman, W. 'Portsmouth Education', typescript study, n.d..

Edwards, E. 'The Poor of Portsmouth and Their Relief, 1820-1850', unpublished dissertation for Portsmouth Polytechnic Diploma in English Local History, 1977.

Esmond, R. *Portsmouth Not So Old*, (Gale & Polden, 1961).

Everett Jayne, R. *The Story of John Pounds*, (London, Epsworth Press, 1925).

Gates, W.G. *City of Portsmouth Records of the Corporation 1835-1927, (Charpentier, 1928)*.

Gates, W.G. *City of Portsmouth Records of the Corporation, 1928-1929-1930, (Charpentier, 1931)*.

Gates, W.G. *City of Portsmouth Records of the Corporation, 1936-7*, (Charpentier, 1938).

Gates, W.G. *Illustrated History of Portsmouth*, (Charpentier, 1900).

Gates, W.G. *Portsmouth and the Great War*, (*Evening News* and *Hampshire Telegraph Co.*, 1919).

Gates, W.G. *Portsmouth in the Past*, (Charpentier, 1926).

Gatt, L.V. 'The Beneficial Society 1754-1933 and its School 1755-1938', unpublished dissertation for Portsmouth Polytechnic Diploma in English Local History, 1982.

Gulliver, D. *Dame Agnes Weston*, (Chichester, Phillimore, 1971).

Harrison, S.E. *Tramways of Portsmouth* (London, Light Railway Transport League, 1963).

Longmate, N. *The Workhouse*, (London, Temple Smith, 1974).

Mearns Fraser, A. *City of Portsmouth Health Report for the Year 1928*

Nicol, J.C. (ed.) *British Association Meeting, Portsmouth 1911: Handbook and Guide.*

Osborne, C.E. *The Life of Father Dolling*, (London, Edward Arnold, 1903).

Pember Reeves, M. *Round About a Pound a Week* (London, Virago, 1979).

Portsmouth 1937: N.U.T. Conference (University of London Press, 1937).

Riley, R.C. *The Industrial Archaeology of the Portsmouth Region* P.P. No.48, 1987.

Riley, R.C. *The Industries of Portsmouth in the Nineteenth Century*. P.P. No.25, July 1976.

Robinson, S. *A Life Record*, (London Nisbet & Co., 1898).

Routledge, K.H. 'Crime and Punishment in Nineteenth Century Portsmouth, typescript study, n.d.

Saunders, W.H. *Annals of Portsmouth* (London, Hamilton Adams, 1880).

Slight, H. *History of Portsmouth*, (3rd edition, 1838).

Stanford, J. and Temple Patterson, A. *The Condition of the Children of the Poor in Mid-Victorian Portsmouth* P.P. No.21, 1974.

Stapleton, B. and Thomas, J.H. (eds.) *The Portsmouth Region*, (Gloucester, Alan Sutton, 1989).

Swenarton, M. *Homes Fit for Heroes*, (London, Heinemann Educational Books, 1981).

Taylor, N.F. 'The Effects of War on Education in Portsmouth 1939-1942', unpublished thesis for the College of Education 1972.

Thompson, P. *Portsmouth Borough Gaol in the Nineteenth Century*, P.P. No.33, 1980.

Weston, A. *My Life Among the Bluejackets*, (new and revised edition London, Nisbet & Co., 1915).

White, L. *The Story of Gosport*, (new and revised edition, edited by L. Burton and B. Musselwhite, Southampton, Ensign Publications, 1989).

Winton, J. *The Naval Heritage of Portsmouth*, (Southampton, Ensign Publications, 1989).

Sources and Notes

Introduction

1. W.G. Gates, *Illustrated History of Portsmouth* p.486.
2. *Ibid.* pp.487-8, quoting G. Pinckard.
3. *Ibid.* p.531.
4. W.H. Saunders, *Annals of Portsmouth* p.189.
5. W.G. Gates, *City of Portsmouth Records of the Corporation, 1835-1927* p.29.
6. PCRO 16A/143 Newspaper cutting, 30 August 1842, found in the notebook of Captain James Anderson, R.N. of Westbury House, Titchfield.
7. Saunders, *Annals*, p.126-7.

PART I:

1. Gates, *Records, 1835-1927*, p.35.
2. J. Stanford and A. Temple Patterson, *The Condition of the Children of the Poor in Mid-Victorian Portsmouth*, p.3.
3. Gates, *Records, 1835-1927*, p.63.
4. *Ibid.*, p.84.
5. *Ibid.*, pp.185-6.
6. R. Esmond, *Portsmouth Not So Old*, p.4.
7. *Ibid.*, p.2.
8. W.G. Gates, *City of Portsmouth Records of the Corporation, 1928-1929-1930*, p.xxi.
9. Gates, *Records 1835-1927*, p.225.
10. PCRO 182/A/3/10 Official Representation of MOH under Housing of the Working Classes Act November 1909.
11. PCRO AP200 Housing of the Working Classes Act, 1911.
12. *British Association Meeting, Portsmouth 1911: Handbook and Guide*, p.147.
13. M. Swenarton, *Homes Fit for Heroes*, p.189.
14. *Ibid.*, p.8.
15. Gates, *Records 1835-1927*, p.283.
16. PCRO DV/9B/1 Unfit Housing.
17. Gates, *Records 1928-1929-1930*, p.63.
18. *E.N.*, 6 January 1934.
19. W.G. Gates, *City of Portsmouth Records of the Corporation, 1936-1937*, p.10.
20. *E.N.*, 7 May 1934.
21. *E.N.*, 18 January 1973.
22. *E.N.*, 21 November 1980.
23. *H.T.*, 15 June 1901.
24. W. Besant and J. Rice, *By Celia's Arbour: A Tale of Portsmouth Town*.

PART II:

1. Gates, *Illustrated History*, p.606.
2. R.C. Riley, *The Industries of Portsmouth in the Nineteenth Century*, P.P. No.25, 1976, pp.6-7.
3. *The News*, 27 November 1955.
4. *Ibid.*
5. B. Stapleton and J.H. Thomas (eds.), *The Portsmouth Region*, p.115.
6. Stanford, *Condition of the Children*, p.14.
7. *The News*, 5 January 1978.
8. *Kelly's Directory of Portsmouth and Southsea, 1903* and *1931-1932*.
9. J. Cramer, 'Messrs. Treadgold of Portsea Town', dissertation for Portsmouth Polytechnic Diploma in English Local History, 1982.
10. M. Pember Reeves, *Round About a Pound a Week*, p.21.
11. Department of Employment, *British Labour Statistics*, p.41.
12. T. Barfoot, 'Portsmouth and the Great War', typescript study, n.d., Appendix A, p.80.
13. *Portsmouth 1937: N.U.T. Conference*, pp.30-32.

PART III

1. See *Introduction*.
2. Stanford, *Condition of the Children*, pp.4-5.
3. R. Rawlinson, *Report to the General Board of Health on the Sewage, Drainage and Water Supply of Portsmouth*, 1850.
4. Stanford, *Condition of the Children*, p.6.
5. L.V. Gatt, 'The Beneficial Society 1754-1933 and Its School 1755-1938', unpublished dissertation for Portsmouth Polytechnic Diploma in English Local History, 1982, p.15, quoting M.G. Jones, *The Charity School Movement*, 1938, p.4.
6. W. Durman, 'Portsmouth Education', typescript study, n.d., p.179.
7. R. Everett Jayne, *The Story of John Pounds*.
8. The Home was still in existence at the time of the John Pounds Centenary celebrations, and in 1941 was evacuated to Newport, I.O.W.
9. PCRO 11A/30/16 A Personal Inspection of the Schools . . . in Relation to Public Health, Henry Slight, 1851.
10. Gatt, *op.cit.*, p.77.
11. Beneficial Society Laws and Regulations, 1829, preface.
12. PCRO New ref. no. not available, Portsmouth and Portsea Free Ragged Schools, 1861-1862: Report.
13. Gates, *Records, 1835-1927*, p.119.
14. PCRO DS 32/1-2. Portsmouth and Portsea Free Ragged Schools Log Book, 1875-1893.
15. Mrs. Ford held the post of mistress.
16. PCRO DS 32/1-2 Log Book.
17. R. Esmond, *Portsmouth Not So Old*, p.37.

18. PCRO 11A/22/16 Transcription of Henry Slight's Report on the Day and Sunday Schools in Orange Street.
19. Durman, 'Portsmouth Education', p.50.
20. *Ibid.*, p.208.
21. PCRO DS/18/10 Kent Street School, H.M.I. Report.

PART IV
1. W.G. Gates, *Records, 1835-1927*, pp.36-7.
2. *Ibid.*, p.47.
3. PCRO 16A/143.
4. K.F. Carpenter, 'Public Health in Portsmouth, 1873-1900', unpublished dissertation, Faculty of Education Studies, Portsmouth Polytechnic, 1979, Appendix 1.
5. PCRO CCM9 Minutes of the Urban Sanitary Committee.

PART V
1. Quoted by N. Longmate, *The Workhouse*, from G. Crabbe, *The Poetical Works of George Crabbe*.
2. Longmate, *op. cit.*, p.270.
3. *Ibid.*, p.270.
4. Gates, *Illustrated History*, p.375.
5. PCRO 193A/1/1/1/1-68, Minute Books of 1838-1846.
6. Longmate, *op. cit.*, p.88.
7. PCRO/W3 Porter's Admissions and Discharge Book, 1937-1940.
8. PCRO BG/W2 1879-85 Creed Register.
9. PCRO BG/M1/32 Overseer's Minutes 1900.
10. PCRO 570/A/6 Rules re Diet, 1900.

PART VI
1. K.H. Routledge, 'Crime and Punishment in Nineteenth Century Portsmouth', typescript study, n.d..
2. Gates, *Records, 1835-1927*, pp.63 and 66.
3. PCRO CCM 1/1-2 Watch Committee Minutes.
4. PCRO S21 Police Evidence.
5. PCRO PCRO 57/2 Calendar of Quarter Sessions 1854-1862.
6. PCRO S9(Z) Deposition of Thomas Plummer Boyle.
7. PCRO 7/2 Calendar of Quarter Sessions 1854-1862.
8. *H.T.*, 14 April 1966.
9. *News*, 1 August 1980.
10. *News*, 31 July 1980.
11. *H.T.*, 17 November 1922.
12. *News*, 13-14 March 1974, reprint of original articles.

PART VII

1. H. Slight, *A Chronicle History of Portsmouth*, p.6.
2. Gates, *Illustrated History*, p.557.
3. PCRO 11A/30/6.
4. Durman, *op. cit.*, p.72.
5. PCRO 449A/2 Portsmouth Brotherhood Boot fund, and *News*, 27 January 1937.
6. *The News*, 19 September 1933.
7. S. Robinson, *A Life Record*.
8. A. Weston, *My Life Among the Bluejackets* and D. Gulliver, *Dame Agnes Weston*.
9. R.R. Dolling, *Ten Years in a Portsmouth Slum*.
10. *Ibid.*, p.11.
11. *Ibid.*, p.29.
12. *Ibid.*, p.139.
13. *Ibid.*, p.145.
14. C. Osborne, *The Life of Father Dolling*, p.163.
15. Dolling, *op. cit.*, p.176.

PART VIII

1. *Southern Daily Mail*, 17 October 1896.
2. W.G. Gates, *Portsmouth in the Past*, p.75.
3. Saunders, *Annals of Portsmouth*, p.203.
4. Chamberlain's *Portsmouth Directory, 1881-82*, p.74.
5. *H.T.*, 11 May 1901; 1 June 1901.
6. *H.T.*, 3 November 1966.

. . . and Conclusion

1. S.E. Harrison, *Tramways of Portsmouth*, p.87.
2. *The News*, 7 June 1989, letter from Ted Williams.
3. N.F. Taylor, 'The Effects of War on Education in Portsmouth 1939-1942', dissertation for Portsmouth College of Education 1972, p.18.
4. G.E. Barnett and V. Blanchard, *City of Portsmouth Records of the Corporation, 1936-45*, p.110.
5. *The News*, 25 March 1972.
6. PCRO 1514A/1.

Abbreviations

EN   Evening News
HT   Hampshire Telegraph
PCL   Portsmouth Central Library
PCRO   Portsmouth City Records Office
PP   The Portsmouth Papers
PPL   Portsmouth Polytechnic Library

Acknowledgements

My most sincere thanks are due to Dr. J.H. Thomas, School of Social and Historical Studies, Portsmouth Polytechnic, for his invaluable comments and criticism.

I would also like to acknowledge the assistance of the members of staff at the Portsmouth Records Office and Portsmouth Central Library; Mrs. Jill Penny, Central Photography Unit, Portsmouth Polytechnic, and Mrs. Lesley Burton, City Architect's Office; Ms. Brenda Jacob, Head Librarian at *The News*. Thanks too for the invaluable support provided by Brian Patterson and the Portsmouth Royal Dockyard Historical Society. Many thanks also to Mr. Deane Clarke, and those residents of Portsea who so kindly contributed first-hand memories of pre-World War II Portsea. Michael Southcott painted the dust jacket illustration, and I am grateful to him for agreeing to contribute to the book.

And finally, my thanks are to due to my Michael . . .

JOY HARWOOD
November 1990

→ *Portsea, 1933.*
(PCRO)

Index